MW01293627

AMAZING GRACIE

MICHAEL HAIBACH

Copyright © 2018 by Michael Haibach

ALL RIGHTS RESERVED. No part of this book may be reproduced or transmitted in any form by any means, electronic or mechanical, including photocopying and recording, or by any information storage and retrieval systems, except as may be expressly permitted in writing by the author or publisher. Requests for permission should be addressed to MJH Publishing, via email at:

MJH@amazing-gracie.com

First Edition, March 2018

MJH PUBLISHING
LOS ANGELES

This work depicts actual events in the life of the author. It is inspired by and based on a true story. Some characters names and have been changed for their protection. Any resemblance to actual persons, living or dead, are purely coincidental.

ISBN: 978-1981923083

Printed in the United States of America

10 9 8 7 6 5 4 3 2 1

This book is inspired by and dedicated to my grandmother:

GRACE MARY DODSON HAIBACH

1893 – 1996

With special thanks to
Leslie Jacobs and Carla Malden

PROLOGUE

I thought I knew my grandmother's story by heart. She had told it many times, each time with the same well-rehearsed delivery: poised, articulate, and consistent, with just enough emotion and attention to detail. No one ever questioned her, not even her family.

My grandmother, Grace Mary Dodson Haibach, had it all: money, social position, a loving family, and a peerless pedigree. Her large house in the prestigious neighborhood of Los Feliz was surrounded by beautiful gardens full of roses and pink carnations. Gardening, in fact, was one of her passions, and keeping an immaculate, well-run house was part of her longstanding routine.

Her manner and ways were formal, and she observed formalities that seem quaint by today's standards but were commonplace a century ago. Her appearance was perfect in every way, from the style of her hair to her color-coordinated dresses and shoes. When she went to church every Sunday, her hats always matched her dress. But no one knew the real facts of her life, the secrets she had kept locked up for almost a hundred years. Not even her closest family members knew that she was not who she said she was.

My grandmother's story begins on a train. How she came to be on that train to the city of her nightmare childhood is a true story, the story of a woman whose transcendent life was more tragic, more courageous, and more unexpected than fiction.

CHAPTER ONE

<u>Pennsylvania, 1913</u>

Out of the soothing, repetitive motion of the train came a nightmare, and out of the nightmare came voices – some soft, others loud and frightening and insistent.

> *Do not talk to any guest in the house, unless the guest addresses you first!*
>
> *What's that in your pockets, child?*
>
> *Just pretend you're me. You play me better than I do myself.*
>
> *Your little brother Jimmy is dead.*
>
> *Why do you do that? Look down at the floor all the time.*
>
> *How's my special little girl?*
>
> *Your father's a murderer and your mother's a...*
>
> *Give me those leg braces. No one will adopt a crippled child.*
>
> *Go on, children... say goodbye to your mother.*
>
> *Tell me about you, Gracie. I want to know everything.*

Grace's eyes snapped open. She had fallen asleep sitting upright in a first class compartment on the train. As the locomotive jolted to a stop, she saw the sign above the station: Welcome to Erie.

She was on her way to meet the man she loved, and he had made all her travel arrangements; all she had to do was pack and get herself to the train station in Pittsburgh. But when she arrived at Station Square, the terminal for the Pittsburgh & Lake Erie Railroad, she had no idea where to go. She had only taken a train once before, but that trip had been three years ago, under cover of night, and no one had made any arrangements.

Grace stood on the platform, a gloved hand to her lips, wondering which direction to take. She saw a line of people and joined it, smiling at the other passengers as she gently set down her two borrowed suitcases. A few of them were looking at her strangely. She glanced down at herself; the full-length charcoal grey hobble skirt, lace blouse, and beribboned jacket that matched the ribbons in her skirt were all in place. Still the other passengers gave her unnerving stares that seemed more like glares.

She touched her hair nervously. She had twisted up her thick pale-gold locks under a wide-brimmed hat trimmed with pheasant feathers that matched the ribbons in her skirt and jacket. Grace was naïve; the wonders of a fine wardrobe were still new to her. She hadn't realized – until now – that her elegant clothes set her apart.

I'm one of you. I'm just a maid! She wanted to let them know she was a working person, too.

A railway porter approached. "Excuse me, Madame."

Grace did not respond.

"Madame? Excuse me," the porter said, a little more loudly.

Grace stood quietly watching the other passengers, who continued to sneak glances at her.

The porter tapped her on the shoulder.

Grace spun around, startled. "Me? Sorry! Yes?" No one had ever called her *Madame* before.

"I'm quite certain, Madame, you're in the wrong place. May I see your ticket?"

Grace was embarrassed by her own ignorance. "I...I... I don't have one," she stammered. "A friend made the arrangements for me."

The porter glanced at his clipboard. "What's the name, Madame?"

"Grace."

The porter's eyebrows rose as he peered at her over his horn-rimmed spectacles. "Your surname, Madame."

The knot in Grace's stomach tightened. "Dodson. I'm sorry. Grace Dodson." She tried to smile.

The porter ran down his list. "I don't have a... Oh, is that D-a-w-d-s-o-n?"

"Yes!" A quick breath of relief escaped her lips.

The porter became officious. "As I suspected, you are in first class. If you will follow me, please, I will escort you to your compartment."

As she bent down to pick up her suitcases, the porter tooted his whistle, and another porter materialized to pick up the luggage.

"This way." The first porter led her to the car marked First Class; the luggage porter followed behind.

"Here we are, Miss Dawdson – your private compartment."

Grace almost gasped: the compartment was as big as her bedroom.

"Enjoy your trip, Madame," said the porter, handing her a ticket.

As she fumbled in her purse for coins to tip the men, the main porter said, "No, no. Mr. Haibach has taken care of everything."

Mr. Haibach had indeed taken care of everything: the private compartment in the first class car was luxurious. She had only ever seen such fine upholstery in the home where she worked as a maid. Grace removed a glove and ran her hand over the rich fabric. She couldn't believe this whole room was *just for her*. Through the window she could still see the line of passengers she had been standing with minutes before. *They are still waiting*, she thought, *and I am already comfortably seated*. Her first impulse was to wave them in to join her – there was so much room in her first class compartment. She felt a twinge of guilt.

The guilt passed when she caught sight of the bouquet. On a little table ledge under the large window stood a small vase filled with fragrant pink flowers. She wondered if all first class compartments came with flowers in her favorite color. An envelope lay next to the vase. *For me?* She pulled out the note card and read:

> *Gracie,*
> *I can't wait to see you. Don't be nervous, my family doesn't bite.*
> *I will be waiting for you at the train station when you arrive.*
> *Enjoy your trip.*
> *John*

Grace did enjoy the trip. It was amazing to watch the green

countryside flow by as she looked out the big picture window. *Pennsylvania really is quite beautiful,* she thought to herself. The scenery moved faster and faster as the train picked up speed. It occurred to her that, like the train, she was rocketing forward on a course and at a speed she could not stop. *How did I get here?* Never mind, she told herself. The spectacle of the ever-changing views outside her window absorbed her and soon the vibration of the moving train lulled her into a state of serenity, and finally to sleep. Until the relentless voices in her head woke her up.

What if someone recognizes me? What if they try to send me back to the orphanage? Oh, how I wish Meg were here!

Grace reached for her hat and plopped it on her head. Almost immediately she heard a gentle, friendly voice – Meg's voice. Whether she imagined it or not, she knew her dearest friend was with her on that train. "Put your hat on gently, my dear. Don't muss your hair."

With great care and slow deliberate movement, Grace lifted the hat off her head and placed it back on the seat. Then, as if she were Meg, she smoothed her hair and ever so elegantly placed it back on her head. Just as Meg would have done.

CHAPTER TWO

Since the night John and Grace had met, she had shared few details about herself and her past. She had never told him she'd lived in an orphan asylum. Quite the contrary: she had led him to believe that her parents had been well-to-do Boston clothiers who had died in some tragic way, leaving their only child to live with an aunt in Pittsburgh. John was a gentleman; he didn't pry or ask too many questions. Her extraordinary beauty, her wide-set slate blue eyes, clear complexion and winning smile were enough to make him fall in love. And now the time had come for Grace to meet his family.

"Gracie!" As soon as she stepped off the train, she heard his voice. She turned to see John walking quickly toward her through the crowd. He was still the most handsome man she had ever seen, with dark wavy hair and dark caring eyes that seemed to look right through to her very soul. When she raised her head from beneath her wide-brimmed hat, the sunlight lit her face and she smiled.

As their eyes met, she almost thought she heard him cry out with delight. Her heart was racing as she tried to hold her composure; she had almost forgotten what a good-looking man he was. Seeing him now, she was once again captivated. She took a deep breath as he raced toward her.

"John, it's so good to see you," she beamed. She extended her hand, expecting him to kiss it gallantly as he'd done before. Instead, he pulled her toward him and gave her an affectionate kiss on the cheek. Her heart skipped a beat; she felt dizzy and nearly lost her balance. John's strong hands steadied her and the color rose in her face.

"Welcome to Erie," he said. "You look beautiful!"

Grace just smiled, aware of the heat in her blushing cheeks.

"How was the train ride? I hope it wasn't too tedious for you."

"No, on the contrary," she replied. "It was wonderful. I don't know where the time went."

"I hope you slept some. I always do on trains. I think it's the vibration; it puts me to sleep every time."

Grace realized she'd been twirling one of the little pink flowers from the vase in her compartment. She had wanted a memento to mark the first flowers she'd ever been given and had put one in her purse, along with John's card. Then she'd pulled another one from the vase to inhale its sweet fragrance. She was still holding that flower when she stepped off the train.

"Thank you for the lovely flowers. They are absolutely divine," she said as she lifted it to her nose and gazed into John's eyes. "So fragrant, and my favorite color, too. No one has ever given me flowers before. What kind are they?"

John looked at her oddly. "Why, they're carnations. And I find it hard to believe that no one has ever sent you flowers. You are more than welcome, and I can assure you there will be plenty more flowers in your future, especially pink carnations."

"Yes, carnations are my favorite," Grace smiled, holding it out to him. "This one's for you."

He placed it in the buttonhole of his lapel. For a moment their eyes met, and Grace felt her cheeks growing warm again. She busied herself adjusting the carnation.

"Very nice," she said, giving his lapel a little tap. Then she made a mental note: *pink carnations;* she had not heard of them before. The flower looked perfect against his brown pinstripe suit.

"I hope you don't mind, but I've taken the liberty of planning our weekend," said John, as he opened the door to his Ford touring car. Another first! Not only had Grace received flowers from this man, she was about to ride with him, for the first time – just the two of them – in his fine automobile!

"Not at all. It sounds lovely," she said as she settled into the seat. Actually, she was relieved. The itinerary for the weekend, John explained, would begin with taking the long way home so he could introduce Grace to his hometown. She nodded and smiled and did not mention that she herself had once lived in Erie.

"We'll stop and have lunch by the lake. Then you'll have time to relax and freshen up before we dine with my mother and sisters. And on Sunday, we'll go to morning Mass with my family. After that, we'll have a family picnic in the park and you'll get to meet the whole Haibach clan."

Grace's stomach clenched. *A picnic?! What does one wear to a picnic? Did I pack the right clothes?*

But Grace loved the Erie that John showed her from the moment they left the train station. It wasn't at all like the Erie she had known and grown to hate from inside the orphanage. The weather was warm and balmy with a slight breeze, typical for an early September afternoon in a city by the lake. John pointed out the sights as they drove through the city and then into the countryside and out to the lake. The trees were still green but John explained that in a month they would turn a hundred shades of yellow, orange and crimson.

Lying beneath an old maple tree, amidst a blaze of colorful leaves, had been Grace's favorite place when she was very little. The tree was big and strong and, as her father once explained, always survived, no matter what it had to endure: storms, floods, freezing winters, hot, dry summers. It had even survived being struck by lightning. She liked that about the sturdy old tree. It became her special place and her friend – strong, yet graceful. It was her second most favorite place in the whole world.

"Gracie!" her father would call as he approached their cabin from the road. "How's my special little girl?" His voice was deep and comforting and when she heard it, she would light up like Christmas morning. No one else in her family could figure out how, at three years old, she knew exactly what time it was, but every day she insisted on sitting under that tree just before five o'clock to wait for her Poppa to come home. And when he got close enough, she would run and jump into his arms, her *first* most favorite place in the whole world.

"Gracie, did I lose you?"

John touched her arm. She stared at him blankly. "I said you'll have to come back in a few weeks to see the fall colors."

The image in her mind faded and she focused on his face. Oh, how she loved to look at him! "That would be lovely," she said. *He must think me utterly mad*, she thought to herself.

9

John flashed her a smile as he maneuvered the car up a narrow road that led to a long driveway. At the end of the driveway stood a stone house, two stories tall, and surrounded by tall trees and carefully trimmed hedges.

The Haibach family home was large, inviting and comfortable. Grace liked the way the house felt – welcoming and not formal. The furniture looked as if it had served generations. Solid and dark, the tables, chairs and cabinets might have been carved from ancient trees in the Black Forest. Grace smiled as she looked around; she liked the look of permanence about the place. It had been a long day and she had less than two hours to settle in, refresh for supper and somehow try to relax and prepare herself for meeting John's mother and twin sisters. She had braced herself to meet them when John drove up to the house, but fortunately for her, his mother had retired for her afternoon nap and the sisters were out shopping.

"They are probably worried about what to wear to meet you, Gracie," said John. "I may have mentioned something about your great fashion sense."

Grace smiled, hoping they wouldn't be disappointed, but mostly at the irony that she had any "fashion sense" at all. The clothes she wore weren't hers.

CHAPTER THREE

Before she met John Haibach, the last perfect day Grace Dodson remembered was the first of September, 1896. That was the day before her world began to unravel. She was sitting in the gold and crimson leaves beneath the maple tree, waiting for her Poppa to come home.

The Dodson family's cabin was small, but the property on which it sat was large, thirty-eight acres of mountainous woodlands in Jefferson County in the middle of Pennsylvania. Grace's grandfather had owned the property since his father, Grace's great-grandfather, had emigrated from England to the United States. The Clarion River ran through the county, and acres of woodlands rich in maple, hickory, hemlock, white oak and beech had given birth to a thriving lumber industry that provided the area's chief source of employment.

William Dodson, Grace's father, called their two-story wood cabin "cozy." There were two small rooms upstairs and two rooms downstairs. The furnishings were sparse but adequate. "One of these days I'm gonna build us a huge house, where each of us will have his own room," he'd tell his family. They were down to five children now. Their two eldest sons, Ashley and Andrew, had been killed in a tragic train accident, trying to outrun an oncoming locomotive, crossing the tracks again and again, each time letting the train get a little closer before jumping out of its way. On the last try of the day, the train won. Ashley was killed instantly, but Andrew lingered for three days before he succumbed to his injuries.

William and Ida were devastated at the loss of their two eldest boys. But in time, more babies came and now there were five Dodson children: William, or "Will," the eldest, just shy of eleven; Rhoda, nine; Rebecca seven; Melinda or "Linnie" as they called her, four; and the youngest was three year-old Gracie, the little girl with the crooked legs.

Gracie was born with a deformity of the legs called *genu varum* – more commonly known as bowleggedness. Most babies are born with some degree of *genu varum*, but usually outgrow it by the age of three. Unfortunately for Grace, her legs remained severely deformed. Her right leg was more bowed than the left, making it function as if it were shorter, although technically they were the same length.

It wasn't long before word of the little girl's condition reached the local authorities, who showed up at the Dodson home, demanding she be fitted with leg braces. This was a hardship and great expense for the family, but they had no choice but to comply, because these same small-town authorities threatened to take little Gracie if her bowlegs were not properly addressed. The awkward metal braces were strapped onto her tiny legs from just above the knee down to her shoes and held tightly in place by thick leather straps. The contraptions were painful to wear and often had to be adjusted and tightened.

But Gracie was an energetic child and, like most three-year-olds, would rather run than walk. At the end of each day, when her father returned home from his job at the lumber mill, he would always wait until he was fairly close before calling out her name. He knew she would be waiting for him under the maple tree. He also knew that once she saw him or even heard his voice, she would jump up and try to dash out to the road to meet him.

"Poppa!" she would scream as soon as she saw him. Then, almost like a mechanical toy, she'd tilt from side to side as fast as she could on her stiff little legs. If her father was not close enough to catch her, she'd end up taking a tumble or two. Gracie never stopped trying to run, in spite of the confounded braces, until her father scooped her up in his arms and showered her with kisses.

"How's my special little girl?" he'd ask, looking up at her against the bright blue summer sky. She was his little angel, flying above him, and he was her beloved protector.

Even with the unsightly braces, Gracie was an extraordinarily pretty child, with curly golden locks and blue eyes that were too big for her chubby little face. Friends and family used to tell her she had the face of an angel, which she got from her mother, and the will and determination of the devil, which she got from her father.

William Dodson was a hard-working man who loved his family more than anything. His deep, dark eyes revealed the gentle soul within. Literate but not well educated, he had left school at the age of twelve and gone to work as a laborer in the lumber mills. He was not a big man, standing a mere five feet six inches and weighing only one hundred thirty-five pounds. He was only forty-one and his hair, once thick and dark, was now grey and thin. Hard labor and caring for a large family aged a man prematurely.

Gracie's mother Ida was thirty-three years old and had already given birth to seven children. She was expecting the eighth, not counting three miscarriages. Being pregnant for most of her married life had aged Ida, too, although she retained traces of the stunning beauty that had first attracted her husband. At the age of sixteen, Ida's father had marched her down the aisle to marry the man responsible for putting her in a family way. William and Ida hadn't minded the shotgun wedding because they were truly in love.

Abstinence was the only form of birth control at the time; William's Catholic upbringing trumped that of Ida's Protestant faith, although neither was particularly religious. They only attended local church services on holidays. Ida was tired of being pregnant but she could never persuade William to stop wanting her. The result was an ever-increasing family.

"Somehow we'll manage, Ida," William would say, whenever she told him she was pregnant again.

"Hi, Pop!" said Will when he saw his father carry little Gracie into the house. Will was sitting in a chair by the stove, his head buried in a book as usual. The smartest of the Dodson clan, Will was determined to amount to something one day and he read everything he could get his hands on and studied every chance he got.

"Hi, Poppa," said Rhoda and Rebecca in unison as they placed dishes and utensils on the dinner table. The two oldest girls were two years apart in age, but they acted more like twins and were inseparable.

William set Gracie down and greeted his children with an affectionate pat on the head.

"Now wait a minute," he said, looking around the room. "Don't I have five children? One's missing. But who?"

This was the game they played every night when Poppa came

home from work. Linnie, a year older than Gracie, liked to play hide and seek. There weren't many places to hide in the small house, but she'd manage to conceal herself beneath a blanket or behind a piece of furniture. She always thought that if she couldn't see her Poppa, he couldn't see her. William always played along.

"It's not Will," he said, pointing at the oldest boy, still engrossed in his book. "It's not Rhoda or Becka." He turned and noticed the old wooden hutch near the stove – it had open shelves on the top filled with dishes and two cabinet doors on the bottom. The doors were closed tight, but all its contents – pots and pans – were piled on the floor. William glanced at Ida; she smiled and gave him a wink.

"Who could be missing? Gracie's over there." Grace was standing in the corner with her hand over her mouth, trying to keep from giggling.

"Ida, do you know which of our children is missing?"

Ida was too busy dishing up stew to play along.

"It's me, Poppa! It's me, Linnie," a little voice said from inside the hutch. Gracie could no longer suppress her giggles. Linnie burst out of the cabinet doors and into her father's arms.

CHAPTER FOUR

The day was a blur of perfect memories – the train ride in her own first class compartment, the pink carnations, the unexpected kiss on the cheek, and an entire afternoon alone with John. *It is so easy to be with him*, thought Grace, as she sat on the edge of the bed. John had given her the first bedroom at the top of the stairs; it had belonged to his sister Teresa, who had recently married. It was a lovely room, furnished with fine sturdy old furniture similar to what she'd seen downstairs at the Haibach house.

John had shown her an Erie she never knew existed. Her fear that someone from the orphanage might recognize her drifted away as she thought about their conversations, which had largely been one-sided – John did most of the talking. She loved to listen to him talk, and even when they were not talking, the silences between them were comfortable. She let herself relax and stretched out on the soft bed. For the first time, she actually knew what it felt like not to be someone's maid. In a little while, she was fast asleep.

By some miracle, Grace awoke in time to dress for dinner in a long-waisted, form-fitting jacket of midnight blue velvet, with collar and cuffs of periwinkle blue satin, and a matching floor-length velvet skirt. Beneath the jacket she wore a white lace blouse that revealed a hint of bare skin at the neckline. Grace was still unaccustomed to wearing such fine clothes. With butterflies dancing in her stomach, she stared at herself in the full-length mirror, checking every last detail to make certain she had assembled the outfit to perfection. As her eyes finally reached the eyes in the mirror, Grace smiled. For it was Meg who was smiling back at her. Grace and Meg both tilted their chins up ever so slightly, their smiles now confident. Grace watched the reflection as Meg carefully added the finishing touch to the ensemble, fastening a single strand of exquisite pearls around her neck. Meg's "good luck" pearls, her gift to Grace.

"Meg," Grace whispered. "Please stay near and help me through this weekend."

A knock on the bedroom door jolted her back to reality.

She quickly glanced one last time in the mirror. Meg was gone and Grace smiled confidently back, pleased with the way she looked.

"Gracie!" John tapped again on the bedroom door. "Are you ready for –"

Grace flung open the door before he could finish.

John appeared speechless. "Blue is definitely your color," he managed, once he'd regained his composure.

"Is it too much? I can change. It will only take me a second."

The admiring look on John's face set her at ease. If he had said yes, she would have had nothing to change into. She had only brought two more outfits with her and still had no idea what to wear to the picnic.

"Don't change a thing. You look absolutely perfect. You know, we usually don't dress this formally for dinner around here, but tonight we're trying to impress *you*."

Grace stepped into the hallway and closed her bedroom door. "Well, Mr. Haibach, you have succeeded. You look dashingly handsome." John wore a three-piece black suit, white shirt, and red and black bowtie.

"Shall we?" John offered his arm, and he and Grace headed downstairs to the parlor. In spite of the compliments, the uneasiness returned and Grace began to feel the little wings beating against her insides. She was greeted by John's sisters, Loretta and Florence – identical twins who did not dress identically or wear the same hairstyle.

"Who's your dressmaker?" asked Loretta. "This is stunning!" Florence nodded vigorously in agreement.

"I warned you, Gracie, don't trust them around your wardrobe," said John.

Grace warmed to the twins immediately. They were close to her age, with dark auburn hair, dark eyes and the handsome features that seemed to run in the Haibach family. "It's a pleasure to meet you both," she said.

"Mother?" called John. "There you are. Everything under control in the kitchen?"

"*Ja, alles ist fein.*"

Mrs. Haibach, the matriarch of the family, was German in every sense of the word. A large, solid woman with strong features and silver hair pulled straight back into a tight bun at the back of her head, she looked much older than her fifty-eight years, and she dressed in a style that was a quarter of a century old. The long charcoal grey gown with its shawl collar and high-necked blouse was matronly and Victorian.

18

But her eyes were deep and kind, like John's, and, like her son, she looked a person straight in the eye when she spoke.

"Gracie, this is my mother. Mother, this is Grace Dawdson."

"Mrs. Haibach," said Grace, extending her hand. "It is such a pleasure to meet you. I have been looking forward to this moment."

I have been having nightmares about this moment would have been more to the point. Grace soldiered on.

"Thank you so much for having me in your lovely house – er, home this weekend."

"*Danke.* Thank you. We are pleased you could join us. Please call me Mary."

Mary took hold of Grace's arm and led her toward the divan, where the twins had already seated themselves.

"Forgive my mother," said John. "She speaks both English and German, usually in the same sentence."

"*Ach*, don't apologize for me," Mary shot back at her son. "*Sprechen sie*... sorry... do you speak German, my dear?"

"I'm sorry, I do not. I understand only a few words," said Grace. *This is not going well,* she thought, wishing the evening were over.

With one swift wave of her hand, Mary signaled the twins to find another seat. Immediately they jumped up from the divan. Mary settled herself and patted the cushion next to her, telling Grace to "*sitzen.*"

"Mother," said Florence, "Grace was about to tell us about her dressmaker."

"*Das ist nicht wichtig.*" The topic was of little importance. "We are hoping to get to know more about you, my dear, and your family.

19

You seem to have put a spell upon my John here."

Mary Haibach, never one to beat around the bush, continued, "We are simple people, strong Catholics. You are Catholic, are you not, my dear?"

Grace nodded. Mary seemed satisfied.

"We are two generations here in this country. We have worked hard, sacrificed much and have done well. Very well." Mary's eyes were fixed on Grace's. "I have nine children. Do you know what it's like to raise nine children under one roof?"

"Yes," Grace murmured, remembering what it was like to live under one roof with a slew of children.

"But I thought John said you were an only child, *nein?*"

Grace could feel her heart beating against the velvet jacket. She prayed Mrs. Haibach could not see any telltale signs of her terror, and yet she could not look away from Mary's eyes. She took a breath and said, "I am. I was just trying to imagine what it would be like to raise nine children. It must have been difficult."

"No, not difficult," Mary replied. "Worrisome, that's what it was – *is*," she corrected herself. "A mother worries."

CHAPTER FIVE

"Gracie! Grace!" called Ida from the cabin's front door. "It's getting chilly out there. Come on in, now, supper's almost ready!" Ida looked out into the gathering dusk to see her youngest girl sitting under the maple tree, facing the road. She had been sitting there for over an hour waiting for her Poppa, straining her neck to see him come up over the little hill. He'd be calling out to her any second now, she just knew it.

"Will!" Ida yelled into the cabin, "Go get your sister." *Lord, that little girl was stubborn.* Ida wiped her hands on her apron and went back to the kitchen where Will sat at the table studying his schoolbook. "You heard me, Will. Go bring Gracie inside."

"Yes, Mama."

When Will left the room, Ida muttered to herself, "Where is that man? I knew it meant trouble, him going off with Frank this morning. That's all it ever is with those two. Trouble. Now I'm going to be up all night trying to get that child to bed."

On account of the leg braces, putting Gracie to bed was a chore and a challenge. As soon as the metal and leather were unstrapped from her legs at bath time, Gracie would run around the house like a little demon. In fact, she wouldn't let Ida or even Will try to catch her, so glad to be free of those uncomfortable restraints. Ida could only

21

watch helplessly as her youngest child dashed around, squealing with joy.

"She'll wear herself out," William would say. But Ida could only shake her head. Gracie never ran out of energy.

"I want to stay up with Poppa!" she'd cry. Then she'd throw a tantrum.

Her poppa was the only one who could calm her down when she was this upset. He'd cuddle her on his lap, rub her little legs and rock her like a newborn. Eventually, Gracie would allow him to strap the braces back on and put her to bed.

Will went outside and found Gracie sitting in a sea of autumn leaves.

"Hey?" he said softly. He sat down next to her and put his hand on hers, but she snatched it away. "Ain't you hungry?"

Gracie shook her head, her eyes full of tears. Brother and sister sat in silence and played with the brilliant colored leaves that blanketed the ground, never taking their eyes off the road.

"They must have found some work today and just got tied up," said Will. "He'll be home soon. How 'bout a piggyback ride?"

"Poppa promised to tell me a story tonight," Gracie whimpered.

"Which one? Not that old woman in the shoe again?"

Gracie stuck out her lower lip and another tear trickled down her cheek.

"I think you know that one better than anyone, Gracie. Tell you what: if he doesn't get home in time to tell you that story before bed, you can tell it to me. I always forget the ending anyway. Deal?"

That got a smile. Gracie nodded and Will stood up. "Come on, climb aboard!" He bent down so she could climb onto his back and they trotted back to the house, Gracie's little braced legs sticking straight out on either side of her brother.

Later that night Gracie awoke to find her father sitting on the edge of her bed.

"How's my special little girl," he whispered

"Where were you Poppa? I waited and waited."

"Shush. Don't wake your sisters."

William kissed her forehead. "Your Uncle Frank and I were out late looking for work."

Gracie heard her mother and uncle's voices coming from downstairs. Her father tucked the bedclothes under her chin. "I'm sorry I didn't get to tell you a story tonight."

"That's okay. I told one to Will. He liked it," Gracie assured him.

"Good. Now get back to sleep. Give me a hug and we'll see you in the morning."

"Night, Poppa," she said as she clung to his neck. Finally, she pulled away and tried to climb out of bed. "I need to say 'night to Uncle Frank."

Her Poppa gently pushed her back onto the pillow. "No, you don't," he said. "You need to go back to sleep. Frank will be here in the morning." He tried to tuck her in, but Gracie squirmed.

"Now you hush and be still and listen to the wind chimes," Frank whispered. He'd made them himself and hung them in the tree outside the upstairs bedroom window, to soothe his fretful little girl.

"It's the sound of tiny angels watching over you."

"Yes, Poppa," Gracie murmured. Before her Poppa could even stand up, she was fast asleep.

Grace's Uncle Frank was William's youngest brother. Only twenty-seven, he was not a family man, nor did he have any intention of becoming one. Extremely handsome, with deep blue eyes and dimples that accentuated his engaging smile, Frank played the field and had a reputation with the local ladies – married or single, he didn't discriminate. With his good looks, dark wavy hair, muscular body and bad boy attitude, he could charm his way in and out of almost anyone's bed. More than once, he had been caught with his pants around his ankles by an outraged husband – narrowly escaping with his life, but not always with his pants. Although fourteen years apart in age, Frank and William were the closest of all their other siblings. Even though Frank was basically a good fellow, the type who wouldn't hurt a fly, he did on occasion stray into questionable situations – all in the spirit of hijinks and good sport. Sometimes he would tempt his older brother to come along. And sometimes, even though William knew better, he too needed an escape from the workaday grind.

As the sun rose over the mountain ridge that Saturday morning in early September of 1896, a voice called out, "Now! Let's get 'em!" The silhouettes of five armed men crouching behind the trees sprang into the light and rushed toward the Dodson cabin. The pounding on the front door awoke the entire family.

Frank, who was fully dressed, was the first to jump up – he'd spent the night on the sofa in the main room. William and Ida rushed from the adjacent bedroom, Ida wrapping herself in a robe and

William, still in his nightshirt, frantically yanking on his pants.

"Open up! This is the constable!"

Ida, William and Frank looked at each other. The constable pounded again, so hard Ida believed the door would split in two. She looked at her husband with fear in her eyes as she unlatched the door. But before she could even open it, the men pushed their way in with their guns drawn.

"William Dodson?" demanded the man in uniform.

"I am William Dodson. What do you want?" Two of the other men grabbed hold of his arms and clapped handcuffs on his wrists.

"What is this about?" screamed Ida, terrified.

"William Dodson," said the constable, "you are wanted for highway robbery and murder."

CHAPTER SIX

Mary Haibach looked hard at Grace, determined to find flaws, if she had any.

"A mother worries," she said again, "To make sure all her children are safe, cared for and loved. With hopes they grow up to make the right decisions. I have these three still at home." She swept her hand toward John, Loretta and Florence. "And I still worry. I still worry about all nine!"

Grace nodded. "Well, this must have been a wonderful home to grow up in. You should be very proud of yourself and your family. I can't wait to meet them all."

Mary Haibach's eyes were still locked onto Grace's, as if she were drilling into her head to find any falseness there.

"*Ja*," she finally said and glanced toward her children for their reaction. All were nodding their heads and smiling in agreement. Mary seemed satisfied, for the moment.

"Now let's eat," she announced. She rose to her feet and took hold of her son's arm before he could reach out for Grace's. As he escorted his mother to the dining room, Mary whispered in his ear, "I like her." John smiled. But then she added, "So far."

Grace found herself flanked by Loretta and Florence; each twin took hold of one of her arms and followed their mother and brother into the dining room.

"So where did you get your exquisite clothes?" Florence whispered eagerly.

"My parents owned a clothiers in Boston. They imported the latest fashions from Paris."

"I told you, Loretta. Paris originals," said Florence.

"Our older sister is a dressmaker here in Erie," said Loretta.

Grace nodded politely but she knew she had to correct this misimpression. "Actually, they're only copies. My parents would create exact copies from the originals and sell them here. Much more affordable that way."

The dining room was large, but unlike the rest of the house, it was quite stark. A large wooden table dominated the room with enough chairs around it to seat Mary, her nine children and several guests. The food was set out family-style on large platters and serving bowls, and Grace thought it smelled absolutely delicious.

When they had all seated themselves, Mary asked Grace to say the blessing.

"I'll do it, Mother," said John.

"No, Grace is Catholic," Mary replied. "She can say the blessing."

This evening was going to be a series of tests. There was no way to sway Mary Haibach from her purpose: to prove to herself that this young lady was worthy of her son.

If there was one thing Grace knew and knew well, it was every Catholic prayer ever written, recited or memorized. She had St.

Joseph's Orphanage to thank for that.

"Bless us, O Lord, and these thy gifts, which we are about to receive from thy bounty through Christ our Lord. Amen."

The others chimed in "Amen," as they each made the sign of the cross.

The food was authentically and totally German: schweinshax'n and schnitzel and two types of sausage (bratwurst and knackwurst), a potato salad that John claimed was completely different from American potato salad because it was served hot, and an abundance of spätzle, or egg noodles.

Dinner started off pleasantly enough, with little conversation other than compliments from Grace on the delicious food. With each bite, she relaxed a little bit more and began to feel a little less nervous. But after three or four bites, Mary resumed her fact-finding mission.

"Tell us about yourself, Grace."

Grace had prepared for this moment, a little like an actress rehearses her part in a play, except the dialogue had not been written. A concocted persona emerged, collected from observation and details and things heard and remembered.

She took a deep breath and realized all eyes were upon her. Exhaling slowly and, she hoped, subtly, she began to speak.

"I would be happy to. I was born in Boston and now I live in Pittsburgh with my aunt and cousin. My parents were clothiers. Mother was active socially but she was just as involved as my father in their business."

Mary Haibach nodded almost imperceptibly in approval. "Go on, dear."

"Well, sometimes my mother would use me as a model. I had to stand for hours while she draped and pinned her fabrics onto me. There were times I felt like a human pincushion."

"She was obviously a talented seamstress," said Florence.

John kept quiet and listened until his mother brought up the very subject he had specifically instructed her to avoid.

"John tells us your parents are no longer with us. I'm so sorry for you. Can you tell us what happened?"

"Mother!" John barked.

Mary Haibach glared at her son and shrugged her shoulders. Her eyes told him she was entitled to hear the truth from the girl's lips.

Grace knew she had to answer. "Yes, they were both killed." She cast her eyes down for dramatic effect; she hoped John's mother would see that the subject was too difficult for her to talk about. But Mary sat silent, waiting for Grace to continue. With her head still bowed, her mind raced. Suddenly she remembered a new arrival at the orphanage, a little girl whose parents had been killed in a train accident, leaving her an orphan at the age of ten. The details of the girl's tragic story came rushing back. Grace raised her head and composed her face into a stoic mask.

"It was in the fall, near Atlantic City." She had no idea then or even now where exactly Atlantic City was, but she kept talking. "My parents were traveling on a passenger train that derailed when it crossed a drawbridge over a channel. The train plunged into the deep icy water."

When the little girl had told this story at the orphanage, she could not stop crying; but today there was no emotion in Grace's voice, nor did her face change expression. She delivered the account in a monotone, as if she were numb from the trauma and tremendous loss. Then she bowed her head and tried to muster a tear, but none came.

"If the fall and impact hadn't killed them, the icy cold water surely would have. Neither of them could swim." She looked up and fixed her gaze on the wall behind Mary, as if reliving the tragedy all over again.

John jumped up from his chair, but his mother raised her hand as if to stop him from consoling her. Grace noticed the exchange. John sat back down and in a soothing voice said, "I remember reading about that accident. It was the Pennsylvania Railroad, one of the worst train accidents in history. More than fifty people were killed and hundreds were injured."

Grace's heart skipped a beat. It had never occurred to her that someone might actually know about that accident. But then, why wouldn't they? It was a true story. She prayed that neither John nor his mother would press her for any further details.

"I'm so sorry, my dear," said Mary. Her voice was low and full of concern. "You are lucky you had an aunt to take you in. Orphanages, I hear, are terrible places for children."

You have no idea, thought Grace. *And please don't ask me any more questions!*

Mary rose from the table. "Let's have our strudel in the parlor, shall we?" She took Grace by the arm. "John, I think we could all use a brandy."

That night Grace fell asleep almost as soon as she put her head on the pillow. This may have been due to the brandy; she'd never tasted it before and even though she had drunk a scant half a glass, she felt the alcohol immediately. But once its effect had worn off, she tossed and turned, her mind wide awake. Finally, she gave up trying to sleep. She slipped on her robe and settled into the window seat, pushing open the curtains to let in the moonlight. The gas-lit street lamps cast a yellow glow in the darkness below and made the row of brownstones across the street look like ominous silhouettes against the moonlit sky. The full moon hung large and low and seemed to be caught in the branches of the tree outside her window. Grace listened to the silence of the night, a welcome relief from the voices that kept playing over and over in her head.

CHAPTER SEVEN

"Murder? My husband didn't kill anybody!" Ida Dodson was shaking more in anger than in fright. Her husband's brother Frank was slowly backing away from the intruders.

"Frank Dodson?" demanded the constable.

"Yes?" Frank answered softly. Two of the men grabbed hold of his arms and put him in handcuffs.

"You're both under arrest for the murder of Louis Helman."

"For what? Who?" shouted William. "I don't even know a Louis Helman. I didn't kill nobody and neither did my brother."

"You got the wrong guys," said Frank.

"Well you can tell it to the jury," said the constable. "Come on, boys, move 'em!" And the men pushed William and Frank out the front door.

"My husband's not a murderer!" screamed Ida. "They didn't kill nobody! This is a mistake!" She grabbed William's coat and ran out after them. "At least let him put on his coat!"

William was wearing just his nightshirt and trousers; neither he nor his brother had boots on their feet. Ida watched the constable's men load her husband and brother-in-law into a horse-drawn paddy wagon and lock the doors. Tears streamed down her face when she saw William look out at her through the bars. The driver cracked his whip and the horses pulled the wagon up the road. The rest of the posse followed close behind on horseback, their rifles at the ready.

What had just happened? Ida stood paralyzed under the old maple tree, her head still echoing with the screams and chaos of the shattered morning. Then it dawned on her: the screams were coming from the house. She spun around to see four little heartbroken faces peering out the front window. She had hoped her children hadn't witnessed their father and uncle being hauled away like criminals, but their hysterical sobs said otherwise. The only face missing from the window was Gracie, but Ida could hear her screams rising above the others.

"Poppa? Poppa!"

Suddenly Ida felt sick to her stomach, as if she'd been punched in the gut. She cradled her pregnant belly. *Please God, don't let the baby come now.* Gasping for breath, she stumbled back to the house and grabbed hold of the doorframe to steady herself. Her children stared at her in terror, searching her eyes for comfort and answers... answers she didn't have.

Gracie's screams rose to a pitch that would wake the dead. Ida saw her youngest child sitting at the top of the stairs, sobbing uncontrollable, wailing for her Poppa. In the commotion the other children had all run downstairs and left their baby sister stranded, unable to get down on her own. Now more frantic than ever, Gracie tried to scoot down the stairs on her buttocks, but her leg braces made it impossible. Will ran up the stairs, picked her up and carried her down. Gracie struggled violently to buck free, but Will didn't dare put her down; he was afraid she would try to run after her Poppa. He simply held her and waited in vain for her cries to stop.

The following week, the *Brookville Republican* blasted the news across the front page:

MURDER IN SNYDER TOWNSHIP
Louis Helman Attacked on the Public Highway
And Shot to Death

Wednesday evening of last week, a cold-blooded murder was committed in Snyder Township, the victim Louis Helman, a Jewish peddler from DuBois.

At the time stated, Helman, accompanied by H. Shakespeare, also from DuBois, stopped at the barn of Thomas Hutchinson and after transacting some business with Mr. Hutchinson's family, the pair proceeded leisurely on their way, driving in a common peddler's wagon in which they carried their wares. When they reached the sugar grove that divides the Hutchinson and Kearney farms, two men sprang out of the brush at the side of the road, and with curses and opprobrious epithets they commanded the peddlers to stop, firing several shots from revolvers in their direction.

The article went on to describe how Helman and Shakespeare tumbled from their wagon to the ground and Shakespeare ran to the Hutchinson homestead for help as several more shots were fired. Helman was found bleeding profusely from a bullet wound to the chest. Matthew Hutchison made a hasty search for the highwaymen and then went for a doctor. Helman was conscious when the doctor arrived, but died about fifteen minutes later.

At the turn of the last century, frontier justice was not restricted to the Wild West. In rural areas all over the country, citizens banded together to redress grievances and right wrongs; those who had firearms kept them handy and used them at will. By the time Helman had expired, a large, armed crowd had gathered around the Hutchinson property, including Constable Morey, who organized a posse and sent them out in all directions. Another family by the name of Britton reported seeing two men running across the fields in the direction of the woods: one of the men was bareheaded. It was later reported that a hat had been picked up at the scene of the crime.

The doctor's post-mortem examination showed that the bullet had entered Helman's chest in the region of the heart and passed through a couple of ribs on its way out. The shot had been fired point blank, as Helman's vest was burned and his breast blistered and filled with powder marks. Besides the bullet wound, there were four cuts on the head and one on the forehead; all of the cuts were clear through to the skull.

The *Brookville Republican* story concluded with the findings of the coroner's jury, which, after a "thorough investigation," returned a verdict that, in their judgment, Louis Helman came to his death at the hands of Frank and William Dodson. The Board of County Commissioner offered a reward for the apprehension and conviction of the outlaws which no doubt hastened the search and capture.

"We are not in possession of evidence upon which this criminating verdict was reached but so able a jury as that named would not reach such a conclusion without direct evidence upon which to base it... The Dodsons are not entirely unknown to peace officers of the county, having had some previous experience in the criminal courts, but in this instance they will have to answer for the highest grade of crime known to the law, and it is hoped that justice, tempered with mercy, may be meted out to them if guilty."

For an article published just a week after the murder, it read like a trial, conviction and sentencing. How the Dodsons were implicated and who did the implicating were never made clear.

Ida gave birth a few weeks after William's arrest. They decided to name the baby Jesse James, after the famous outlaw. It was probably not one of William Dodson's better ideas. The family called the little boy Jimmy and little Gracie was delighted to have a baby brother. It was just like having a new doll to play with.

As the weeks turned into months between the arrest and the trial, all the small-town gossip and speculation took its toll on the Dodson family. The children heard the chants every day when they went to school:

"Your father's a murderer! A cold-blooded killer!"

Will got into fights defending his father's honor and was finally expelled from school. For a boy who so loved learning, this was almost too much to bear. Rebecca and Rhoda kept to themselves; once friendly and playful during school recess, the girls became introverted and talked only to each other. Whenever the family went into town they had to endure finger-pointing, whispers and snubs. Money, which was tight to begin with, was dwindling quickly now that the family's breadwinner was behind bars.

But not everyone believed in William and Frank's guilt. There was a strong contingent of the female citizenry who lined up outside the jail in protest of what they believed was the brothers' wrongful arrest. Or perhaps they were just hoping to get a glimpse of Frank, the handsome outlaw. The local newspapers sensationalized the Dodson Brothers' murder at every opportunity, covering every detail of their arrest, their days behind bars and the upcoming trial. When the papers printed that William had named his newborn son Jesse James, the town roared again in outrage, convinced he had to be guilty.

Ida was stuck at home to nurse the new little "outlaw." As often as she could, she prevailed upon William's sister Annie to watch the younger children. Annie was known as a tough cookie and expert markswoman; her nickname was Annie Oakley and many said she was the best shot in the state. Ida trusted her children to Annie's care when she had to make long trips to neighboring townships to find housework jobs. As word spread of her relationship to the notorious outlaws, she had to go farther and farther away from home to earn a few dollars to support her children. None of the local people would employ her. Caring for the young ones fell to Rhoda and Rebecca, and Will, who was only ten, did the best he could to find odd jobs after school. A life that hadn't been easy to begin with became even harder.

"It'll be all right," Ida tried to reassure her children. "Your

Poppa and Uncle Frank didn't kill nobody and the jury will say so. We'll all be back together soon." But the stress was wearing on her and she began to get headaches. Sometimes she'd yell at the children; her patience was all but gone. In fact, when Ida got so angry, Gracie didn't know what to do. Sometimes all she could do was cry.

Public sentiment, however, was leaning towards the Dodson brothers' innocence. By the middle of November, Ida dared to believe that all would be well. But when it was announced the trial would begin the week before the Christmas holiday, all hell broke loose.

CHAPTER EIGHT

Grace could hear the leaves rustling outside her window in the Haibachs' upstairs bedroom. The bright full moon had sunk a little lower behind the tree as she sat in the window seat looking out, as though the moon were also tired but not yet ready for sleep.

Had tonight gone well? she asked herself, running over every detail, every word Mary Haibach had said to her and every answer Grace had offered to the questions she was not expecting. When John had walked her up to her room, he'd whispered reassurance in her ear and kissed her good night on the cheek.

Maybe it had gone well. After they had finished their brandy and strudel, Mary Haibach gave her a hug – an unexpected gesture from this proper, formal matriarch. It caught Grace by surprise; she could not remember the last time she'd received a hug from anyone. Unaccustomed to signs of affection, she stiffened like a toy soldier. Grace allowed herself a little smile, wrapped her robe more snugly and let herself relax into the soft cushions. Her eyes closed but she did not really sleep.

Before she knew it, sunlight was streaming in through the bay window and she awoke to find herself still in the chair. It dawned on her that in a few hours she would be attending Sunday mass in Erie.

This would be the first time she had actually been inside a church since she had escaped from this very city. It was not the church that she feared, nor had she turned against God or her religion; she prayed her rosary in private every day. What she did *not* want to see were any priests or nuns; the memory of how they had treated her was too awful. And most of all, she was afraid of being recognized.

Grace dressed with care. The quandary of what to wear to a picnic could really only be settled with her one remaining ensemble, a forest green skirt of lightweight wool that allowed more freedom of movement than the hobble skirt she had worn to the train station. Underneath the matching wool jacket, she wore a high-necked silk crepe blouse the color of pale jade. She prayed this would be appropriate picnic wear. And she prayed she would survive Sunday Mass without seeing anyone she had known at the orphanage.

Although John had not specifically asked Grace to join his family in Holy Communion, he had implied it would make a good impression on his mother if she did. Mary Haibach was unyielding on this matter; she expected her family to receive Communion each and every Sunday without fail. It was her way of ensuring that her children were living up to their Catholic upbringing.

When the time came for the family to stand up and file down the center aisle towards the altar, hands clasped in the attitude of prayer, Grace did so as well. She followed behind Mrs. Haibach, and John and his sisters followed behind her. When it was her turn to kneel at the altar, she closed her eyes tightly. She did not dare look into the face of the priest as he placed the consecrated wafer on her tongue. Again following Mrs. Haibach's lead, the entire family rose as one body to return to their pew. As Grace turned up the side aisle, she saw a nun in full traditional habit seated at the end of the first row. The nun's eyes locked on hers. Grace was certain she recognized the sister and even more certain the sister had recognized her.

But what could she do? She had to keep walking forward. With each step she became more convinced the nun was from St. Joseph's Orphanage and had recognized her as a runaway. Panic rose in her chest. As she passed within inches of the woman in the black habit, the nun smiled at her. All Grace could do was nod; her heart was pounding so fiercely, she could not manufacture even the tiniest smile in return. She finally made the turn into the Haibachs' pew. It seemed like the longest few steps of her life.

She knows me. What shall I do now? Her first impulse was to bolt from the church. John, sitting next to her, sensed something was wrong and turned his face to her. When their eyes met, he smiled and that was enough to take her mind off the nun, at least for a few moments; his smiles had that effect upon her. But as soon as he turned away, she felt her heart pounding again.

When Mass was over, Mrs. Haibach led her family from the church, as she did every Sunday, pausing on the front steps to exchange a few words with the parish priest. Grace's heartbeat had slowed and she breathed more easily, knowing she and the family would soon be away from the church. Then she felt a tap on her shoulder. She spun around and found herself face to face with the nun from the first row. Grace knew it was all over.

"Good morning," said the nun. "I'm Sister Anne."

Grace's ears filled with the white noise of panic.

"I noticed you at communion," continued the nun, "And I just had to tell you that your outfit is stunning."

"I beg your pardon?" asked Grace.

"Your outfit is absolutely stunning. It almost makes me want to renounce my vows. Just so I could know what it feels like to wear something so exquisite."

Grace was dumbstruck.

"Instead of... well, this," Sister Anne continued. "But please don't tell anyone I said that." Then she winked at Grace and gave her a warm smile.

It took Grace a few seconds to process what had just happened. She was so flabbergasted, she couldn't even return Sister Anne's smile. But John was right beside her, beaming proudly. "Good morning, Sister Anne. May I present Miss Dawdson? Grace, this is Sister Anne."

"Good morning, John," said Sister Anne. "I'm sorry to have intruded. I just had to tell Miss Dawdson how attractive she looks. It is my pleasure to make your acquaintance." She smiled even more broadly at Grace.

Grace finally managed to return the smile. "Thank you, Sister Anne. It's a pleasure to meet you as well." Grace looked the nun directly in the eyes. There was no sign of recognition. None at all.

"May the Lord be with you both on this glorious Sunday," said the nun as she hurried off into the crowd on the church steps.

Grace exhaled with relief. Sister Anne was much too young to have known her at St. Joseph's anyway.

CHAPTER NINE

The Jefferson County Courthouse stood in the center of Brookville. The two-story red brick structure with its white colonial steeple and looming clock tower was the most imposing building in the small Pennsylvania town. The courtroom inside was cavernous, with white walls and polished pinewood floors and matching pinewood spectator benches. Every bench was filled with spectators. The balcony upstairs was filled, too, mostly with women who were already craning their necks to see handsome outlaw Frank Dodson.

Ida had risen before dawn on the morning of December 16th to make the long trip to Brookville. She had not awakened or said good-bye to her sleeping children; the night before she had tried to reassure them their Poppa would be home and they would be a family again. Even though she arrived forty-five minutes before the start of the trial, she was astonished to find that the courtroom was already packed to the rafters. Ida Dodson, the defendant's own wife, had no choice but to stand in the back of the room.

Just before nine o'clock, the crowd began to murmur; the murmur grew into a roar, and over the roar Ida could hear shouts from the balcony, women's voices crying out to free the innocent men. She stood on tiptoe to see an officer slowly lead her husband William and his brother Frank, handcuffed and shackled, toward the front table on the left. The ruckus grew louder and Ida's heart sank.

At the table on the right, just behind the lawyers for the Commonwealth, sat the star witness for the prosecution, a scrawny man with thin, scraggly hair: Mr. Shakespeare, one of the victims, the peddler who had barely escaped the attack with his life.

"Who are *these* guys?" he blurted in a loud voice. The peddler did not recognize the two men on trial.

C.C. Benscoter, Esq., the grey-whiskered lead attorney for the Commonwealth, spun around and barked, "Good God, *you* ought to know those men! You identified them."

Shakespeare stared at the floor in awkward silence. Benscoter brusquely turned back to the front of the courtroom, adjusted his coat and cast his attention upon the two defendants. William was scanning the crowd looking for his wife. Before he took his seat, he spotted Ida standing in the crowd at the back of the room. Their eyes met and a loving smile flew between them; this was the first time they had seen each other since the arrest.

A young woman sitting in the front row followed William's gaze; when she saw Ida smiling back at him, she stood up and beckoned her to come forward and take her seat. Grateful for this rare display of kindness, Ida maneuvered down the center aisle through the crowd to the front row of benches. The throng fell silent as she passed. The woman patted Ida on the shoulder and gave her an encouraging smile before she walked to the back of the courtroom. Ida sat down directly behind her husband as the judge made his entrance.

"All rise," announced the bailiff at the stroke of nine o'clock.

"The trial will now commence in the case of the Commonwealth versus William and Frank Dodson, for the murder of Louis Helman, in Snyder Township, on the 2nd day of September last, 1896. Jurors have been selected, sworn in and are all present. The Honorable Judge John W. Reed presiding."

Judge Reed was a large man made larger by his black robes. "This court is now in session," he said, banging his gavel. "May we hear the opening arguments from the Commonwealth?"

Mr. Benscoter rose from his seat and slowly approached the jury. "Your honor, gentlemen of the jury, and fellow citizens, the Commonwealth intends to prove beyond a shadow of a doubt that the two men seated before you today –" He paused and pointed in the direction of the Dodson Brothers. "– may have set out to simply rob Mr. Helman and Mr. Shakespeare, but when things went wrong, did not hesitate to commit cold-blooded murder. Or, you may conclude from testimony that the defendants had no intention of robbery at all. Their motive was a premeditated crime of hate. Hate against a friendship between two people of different cultures and different religious backgrounds in an area intolerant of such diversity. Mr. Shakespeare, who sits before you today, barely escaped with his life. But Mr. Helman unfortunately did not, and now his children are fatherless."

Benscoter went on for almost thirty minutes, detailing with great precision the movements of the defendants. The longer he spoke, the more his whiskers seemed to stand out on his full face. "It is our contention," he concluded, "that this heinous crime was not a robbery attempt gone wrong, but was, in fact, deliberate and premeditated. And we intend to prove that beyond a shadow of a doubt, in order for you to serve justice and return a verdict of murder in the first degree."

Ida swallowed the lump in her throat and Mr. Benscoter took his seat.

Judge Reed asked for an opening statement for the defense, but curiously, William McCracken, one of the four attorneys for the defense, responded, "Not at this time, your honor. We do reserve our right for opening comments once the prosecution rests."

And so the testimony began. The prosecution called twenty-five witnesses to the stand, to show the route that the victims and the Dodson Brothers had taken from dawn to dusk, how their paths had crossed throughout that fateful day and how they ended up at the same spot at the precise time of the murder. But the testimony was inconsistent: witnesses were uncertain as to the day of the week, the date itself, the times they saw Helman, Shakespeare and the Dodson Brothers, and even the time of the actual murder. The prosecution failed to establish a clear timeline.

Nor was there consensus as to the identity of the defendants. Some witnesses were emphatic that they had seen William and Frank Dodson at the time of the murder. Others admitted they could not provide a positive identification because they were too far away or only glimpsed the men for a few seconds. Several witnesses gave descriptions that did not fit either Dodson brother; they claimed they saw a balding, heavy-set man fleeing on foot.

Witness after witness was examined and cross-examined and as the day wore on, each cast yet another shadow of doubt as to the guilt of the Dodsons. No two witness accounts matched. The defense attorneys grew confident they would be able to establish in the minds of the jurors that the crime had been committed by some other suspicious-looking character or characters who happened to be in the vicinity.

Mr. Shakespeare had been warned he would be taking the stand on that first day of testimony, but when his name was called, he was caught off guard. Silence fell over the courtroom as the man looked around with surprise and confusion on his face. He finally got to his feet and clumsily made his way to the witness stand, his footsteps echoing through the room. Shakespeare looked terrified. Benscoter gave the witness a few moments to calm himself before asking him to state his name, place of residence, occupation and age for the court.

"I'm, uh, twenty-nine years," stammered Shakespeare.

The attorney waited for him to continue but the witness said nothing more. Benscoter took a deep breath and let out a sigh. "State your name."

"H. Shakespeare," the witness replied.

"What does the H stand for, Mr. Shakespeare?"

Shakespeare's gaze snapped away from the crowd and focused on Benscoter's face.

"The H?" repeated Benscoter. "What does it stand for?"

"Nuttin. If it stands for sumpin, ain't nobody told me." Laughter rippled through the crowd. "It's just H."

Benscoter frowned, adjusted his coat and tie and resumed his questioning. "Where, Mr. H. Shakespeare, do you reside?"

"DuBois," said the man.

"And what do you do?"

"I'm a peddler."

"And what do you sell?"

"Dry goods, pots, cooking stuff, and, uh, jewelry."

"How did you know Louis Helman?" asked Benscoter.

"We was partners in bizness, nigh on four years now," replied Shakespeare.

"So, you were business partners... and friends, I presume?"

Shakespeare hesitated, then mumbled something into his lap.

"I'm sorry, I didn't hear you. Please speak up," barked the attorney. "Were you and Mr. Helman friends, Mr. H. Shakespeare?"

The witness cleared his throat. "Yep. We was friends."

Then Benscoter asked the man to describe in his own words the events of the day leading up to the fatal assault. Shakespeare's account, from early that morning through the traumatic events of the afternoon, was spotty, convoluted and unsure, as if he himself could not recall the details of his own whereabouts. Sometimes he would describe a location by naming the owner of the property he and Helman had passed – the Hutchisons' Farm or the Keys' barn – but on several occasions he named a property that wasn't even in the vicinity, but ten or more miles away. Even his description of the assailants, whose paths they had crossed earlier in the day, was full of discrepancies. The further he got into his testimony, the more fidgety he became. When Mr. McCracken, attorney for the defense, began his cross-examination, Shakespeare's hands trembled and his left eye began to twitch.

Both the prosecution and the defense seemed interested in questioning the witness about his friendship with Mr. Helman, who was Jewish; Shakespeare was Protestant. Friendships and associations between people of different faiths were uncommon and even frowned upon in Snyder Township. The prosecution wanted to characterize the murder as a kind of hate crime. But Shakespeare's answers were vague and he spoke utterly without confidence.

When the witness had concluded telling his recollections of the grizzly murder and his own narrow escape, Benscoter posed one final question.

"Mr. Shakespeare, I will remind you that you are under oath to tell the truth and only the truth to this court. I ask you: are the men who assaulted you and killed your friend and business partner, Mr. Helman, in this courtroom today?"

The room was completely quiet. Ida held her breath, confident that his unsure, inconsistent and meandering testimony clearly showed the witness was unreliable. And yet, although just a few hours earlier, Shakespeare had failed to recognize the two defendants, he pointed his finger at the Dodson Brothers.

CHAPTER TEN

Grace may have been overdressed for a picnic, but the Haibach family just assumed it was part of her sophisticated style. Compared to Grace in her forest green ensemble, the other ladies in the party looked rather like plain brown wrens. John's five sisters and older brother, along with their spouses and children, joined Mary, John and the twins at a park by Lake Erie, plus several dozen baskets full of that delicious German food.

"Grace, you must try the chicken," said John's oldest sister. "It's one of Mama's best recipes."

"Yes, yes, and she must try the strudel, too!" cried one of John's nephews.

This is unbelievable, thought Grace. *They are all making such a fuss over me!* "Thank you, yes, it is delicious – No, I've never eaten anything so wonderful – Perhaps one day you might give me the recipe?"

She was pleased with herself that she'd thought of asking for a recipe; that was something Meg might have done. *I'm learning.*

The afternoon went off without a hitch. There was not even one difficult, awkward or uncomfortable question from John's mother or anybody else. Grace was almost positive that John's mother had warned her family not to mention the accident that had killed her parents.

The relaxed small talk and the easy give-and-take among the Haibach clan were a new experience for Grace.

I like this; I could get used to this. This is what it feels like to be part of a family.

During the afternoon Grace noticed John and his mother wander away from the group to have a private and intense conversation. The thought crossed her mind that mother and son were talking about her and she began to worry. But it was such a beautiful day, and all the Haibachs were being so lovely to her... she tried to talk herself out of it. *One bout of paranoia is more than enough for today.*

That evening, as John escorted Grace upstairs to her room, she was seized with an impulse to squeeze his arm.

"Thank you, John, for the most wonderful day. I think today has been the most wonderful day I've ever had in my whole life."

John smiled, staring into her eyes. How she loved to see that smile!

"You're welcome, Gracie," he replied, taking her hand. "I am sorry you have to return to Pittsburgh so soon. Do you think you would mind waking up a little bit earlier tomorrow morning? There's something special I want to do on our way to the train."

Maybe he wants to stop and surprise me with more pink carnations, she wondered.

That night, Grace slept well, better than she could ever remember. No haunting memories, no troubling dreams. In fact, she could not recall dreaming anything at all that night. Perhaps she was at last conquering her fears, one by one.

The train was scheduled to leave the Erie station at half past nine that Monday morning, and the entire Haibach household was up early to see her off. After a hearty breakfast and heartfelt thank-yous, Grace and John were on their way to the station. But instead of stopping at a florist, John took a detour to his favorite spot along the Erie waterfront, a park bench on a green knoll with a view of Presque Isle.

"It's not really an island," he explained as they watched the early morning sun shimmering pink and gold on the lake. "It's a sand spit. But from here it looks like an island."

"It's beautiful," said Grace.

"It is," said John. He took hold of her hand and then spun around, dropping to one knee in front of her. Grace thought he was about to tie his shoelaces. But he looked into her face and gave her the dazzling smile, the smile that always made her forget her worries and believe that all was right with the world.

"Grace... would you consider marrying me?"

Grace's mind went blank.

CHAPTER ELEVEN

Screams and shouts erupted from the balcony of the Brookville courtroom.

"Liar! Liar!"

From the floor came equally zealous shouts that the Dodsons were guilty of murder. William couldn't contain himself; he jumped out of his seat and yelled at Mr. Shakespeare, "That's a damn lie! We didn't kill nobody!"

Shakespeare sunk further down into his chair.

Frank Dodson lowered his head, resting it on his bound arms. Tears cascaded down Ida's cheeks as the pandemonium in the courtroom rose to a deafening pitch.

"Order!" The judge banged his gavel. "Quiet! Order!" He banged his gavel again and again. The town was divided and emotions ran high; Judge Reed's courtroom was the perfect arena for every citizen to speak or shout his piece, and neither man nor woman was ready to be quiet.

But finally, when order was restored, the judge dismissed the witness Shakespeare, who sheepishly returned to his seat in the front row. The Commonwealth rested its case.

After a brief recess, William McCracken, attorney for the

defense, made his opening statement. "Your honor, gentlemen of the jury and fellow citizens," he said, crossing with a measured pace toward the jury box. "Sitting before you are two innocent men, wrongly accused of a crime they did not commit."

He paused and looked at each of the jurors. McCracken was a tall man who seemed aware that his stately presence could be just as influential as his speech.

"Yes, the Dodsons were in the vicinity of the murder on that very day, but they were not at the scene of the murder for a full hour before the shooting took place. The Commonwealth does not have sufficient evidence, and they will not be able to prove otherwise. The Dodsons are also victims here. This is a clear case of mistaken identity."

The attorney paused again and made a three-quarter turn to face the defendants. He gave them an encouraging nod. "William and Frank Dodson may not have stellar records before these courts…" McCracken turned back to face the jury. "But they are not murderers. It is our contention that two unknown persons had followed the peddlers that day – two suspicious characters – and it must have been they who committed this unthinkable crime. The prosecution's evidence, or lack thereof, cannot prove their guilt beyond a reasonable doubt. The jury will have no choice but to return a verdict of acquittal, and allow these two men to go home to be with their families for the Christmas holiday. It is that simple."

He bowed his head respectfully to the jurors and said, "Thank you."

The defense called another dozen witnesses to the stand to

prove that Mr. H. Shakespeare's reputation for truth and accuracy left much to be desired. Then and there, the defense should have rested. But Frank and William Dodson were called to the stand in their own defense. William seemed confused as to the days and times events took place. Frank made matters worse when he told the court that he and his brother had spent that day drinking, buying gun cartridges and shooting for sport by the side of the road. The icing on the cake was his confession that he and his brother had played a prank on a salesman they had met: Frank had introduced his brother as Mr. Stanton Jones and "Jones" had ordered one of the salesman's steam-cooking apparatus. It seemed funny at the time. In a court of law, it sounded like lying for sport and did nothing to support the good character of either defendant.

The circus went on for three full days and gave the spectators and townspeople all the drama and entertainment they had hoped for. Outside the courthouse, people gathered in the streets and shops and scrutinized the conflicting testimony. Most agreed this was far from a clean trial: one member of the jury let it be known he was being pressured to convict. Another witness confessed to being harassed by the arresting officer, Constable Morey, who was in line to collect the reward money himself if the Dodsons were convicted.

And yet no one ever uttered the word "mistrial."

On Saturday, December 19th, the Commonwealth offered their final summation and closing remarks. Every seat in the courtroom was taken and the people who couldn't find seats crammed into whatever space was left. Spectators who couldn't find a place inside crowded onto the courthouse steps. Mr. Benscoter spoke for over two hours;

Mr. McCracken's closing remarks were brief. Each side had delivered its case masterfully and nods of agreement rippled through the courtroom. Public opinion was still equally split.

Judge Reed then presented the jury with its charge. He addressed every discrepancy that had surfaced during testimony and instructed each juror to use his own common sense in evaluating the evidence presented. He urged them to resolve for themselves any conflicts or credibility issues arising from witness testimony.

"It is the opinion of this court," concluded Judge Reed, "that there is no middle ground for you to take in this case, and that your verdict should be either guilty of murder in the first degree, or not guilty... You will now take this case, and in a fearless and honest discharge of your duty, render such verdict as will do justice to the Commonwealth and to the prisoners at the bar."

The judge's recap and final admonition had taken another two full hours to deliver. At the end, everyone was tired and even more confused.

By Christmas Eve, the jurors were exhausted; they had been sequestered for five days and had still not reached a consensus. A conviction of murder in the first degree or an acquittal was expected. But the gentlemen of the jury – five farmers, two laborers, two miners, one merchant, one wagon-maker and one carpenter – rendered a verdict of voluntary manslaughter. It was a compromise and most likely a compromise of convenience.

Counsel for the defense filed a motion in arrest of judgment on a plea of an illegal verdict, along with a motion for a new trial. Judge Reed and the Commonwealth, however, were not disposed to prolong the Dodson matter. William and Frank were declared guilty as charged.

Ida had expected to bring her husband and his brother home that Christmas Eve. Alone and with a hollow heart, she made the long journey back to the cabin from the Jefferson County Courthouse. A heavy snow had begun to fall. Aunt Annie had stayed with the children again that day. With baby Jimmy in her arms, she ran out to road to meet her sister-in-law. The Dodson children watching from the front window saw their mother's downcast face. They could not hear the words exchanged, but the pantomime spoke volumes: Aunt Annie thrust the baby into Ida's arms and tore off down the road.

They never saw Annie, or anyone else from the Dodson family, again.

CHAPTER TWELVE

Ida never spoke her husband's name again. It was Will who told the other children their father wouldn't be coming home.

"They're all crooked – the judge, the lawyers, the jury – Pop and Uncle Frank are innocent." Will had to be strong and stand up for his family: he was the man of the house now.

Ida decided she would carry on with Christmas as usual, but this was difficult for many reasons. She'd made none of the usual holiday preparations because she had been so preoccupied with William's trial. This year, there was no Christmas tree, no decorations, nor had she made any of the special holiday treats that her children loved so much. She was sullen; her moods swung between anger and sadness, resentment and hostility. But she tried to do Christmas for her children.

"Hang up your stockings," she told them. The house had no fireplace, so the family used the coat hooks by the front door. One by one, the children placed their stockings on the hooks before they went up to bed, but there was no joy of anticipation. Ida's somber mood and sorrowful face made sure of that.

As the wind whistled outside and the snow continued to fall, Will overheard Rhoda and Rebecca whispering from the other room.

"Do you think Poppa *did* kill that man?" said Rebecca to her older sister.

"I don't think so," Rhoda whispered back. "Maybe Uncle Frank was showing off again and shot him by accident."

"He never shoots anything by accident. You think they're gonna be hanged?"

Rhoda shuddered. "I don't…"

Before she could finish, Will yelled from the other room, "Pop didn't kill anyone, neither did Uncle Frank. They're all a bunch of crooks, the lot of them. From the constable right down to the judge. All crooks!"

The girls were quiet.

"No one's getting hanged," said Will. "He'll be home soon, when they figure out everyone lied."

For the rest of the night, Will lay awake angry. He was determined not to give up on his father.

Christmas morning, a pall hung over the Dodson house. The children drifted downstairs: first Will, carrying little Gracie, with Linnie close behind. She was holding on tight to his suspenders. Rhoda and Rebecca followed, clutching each other's hand. The five of them stood in a huddle at the bottom of the stairs, like scared rabbits sniffing out impending danger. Ida looked at her children's wary faces. She was embarrassed and ashamed – ashamed that over the last three months she hadn't given them much thought. But she mustered up all the cheer she could and broke the silence. "Merry Christmas, children. Well, go look in your stockings."

For a moment it actually felt like Christmas. The children ran to the coat hooks; their spirits rose and Ida tried to smile. Inside each stocking she had placed a piece of fruit or a handful of nuts, and a special gift that she or William had made for their children. For Rhoda, a hand-crocheted ivory shawl. For Rebecca, a red-beaded necklace. And for Linnie, a hand-sewn rag doll. In Gracie's stocking was an orange and six wooden blocks which her Poppa had hand-carved and painted, just weeks before his arrest.

The blocks spelled G-R-A-C-I-E.

Gracie plopped herself on the floor and turned the blocks over and over. Each side was painted with a different color. She held each block up and traced the carved letters with her chubby little fingers. Will knelt by her side and whispered, "Poppa made those for you."

"Poppa!" Gracie squealed.

"See?" said Will as he lined up the blocks in order. "They spell your name."

Grace loved those blocks instantly. She sat on the floor and played with them for the rest of Christmas day and for many days after that. The very first word she learned to spell was her name.

Will's stocking, however, did not go over well. Ida had had neither time nor energy to make something special for her oldest boy. That was supposed to be William's responsibility. As a last resort, she'd chosen his father's envied pocketknife to be Will's special gift. She thought it would be something her son would cherish; she had nothing else for him. Will stood there, his palm open, the pocketknife resting in the center of his hand like a malignant insect ready to strike. William Dodson had forbidden his children to touch that pocketknife. He'd been very clear about that.

Will looked up at his mother. He searched her face for the meaning of this gift, a gift his father would not approve of. "This is Pop's knife! He wouldn't want me carrying it!"

"Well, he won't be needing it now," said Ida. She couldn't hide the sarcasm in her voice.

How could she? Will thought to himself. *How could she give up on our father so quickly? Did she believe Poppa was guilty, too?*

Will threw the pocketknife on the table, grabbed his coat and ran out of the house and into the snow. He slammed the door so hard it woke the baby.

"What's wrong with Will?" little Gracie called from the floor. Ida stood in the middle of the room, fighting tears, fighting the impulse to run after her son, fighting the headache she could feel coming on.

"Hush," she told Gracie, as she rushed to Jimmy's crib. A screaming infant and a hurt and angry son and no husband… Ida felt like her head was going to explode.

When the baby finally stopped crying, she tried to pull herself together to cook the Christmas meal. She had hoped to talk Will into going out to trap a rabbit or two, or maybe catch a few trout. But now she had to rely on what they had in the house. Luckily, she had plenty of vegetables that she'd canned that summer; in fact, Ida had more than enough tomatoes, snap beans, and squash, plus bushels of potatoes and corn stored in the cool, dark cellar – enough to get the family through a long winter.

Soon the house was filled with the mouthwatering aroma of cornbread cooking in the cast iron skillet and a large pot of vegetable stew. Ida had prepared more than the family needed, along with a pot of hot spiced apple cider. On Christmas Day, it was customary for family, friends and neighbors to stop by to exchange greetings. But this Christmas, no one came.

All of the Dodsons' friends from the neighboring farms – all the people who had believed in William and Frank's innocence before the verdict – stayed away. Ida tried to put on a brave face as she served up stew and cornbread to all of her children, except Will. Her oldest boy finally came home when Ida was washing the dishes. There was still plenty of warm stew in the pot on the stove, and she put a plate on the table for him. Will's face was red – from crying or from the cold, Ida could not be sure.

"Eat, son," she said. "You must be hungry."

Will took a few bites and realized how hungry he was. He scooped up every morsel of stew, wiped his mouth with his sleeve, and went to the pot for seconds.

"There's so much left!" he said. "Who all came over today?"

"Nobody," said Ida.

Ida's thoughts turned dark as she watched her son pick at his second helping of stew. *The whole county thinks the Dodson Brothers are guilty... I wonder.*

CHAPTER THIRTEEN

CONVICTS SENTENCED

On Saturday afternoon, January 9th, Judge Reed imposed the following sentences on prisoners convicted at the December term of court: William and Frank Dodson, convicted of voluntary manslaughter; sentenced to be confined in the Western State Penitentiary for a term of twelve years.

. . . . .

"Page six," said Will as he angrily tossed the newspaper at his mother. Ida grabbed the crinkled copy of the *Jefferson Democrat*.

She read and re-read the brief article. *So now it's final*, she said to herself. Their appeal was denied, and the Dodsons family's last snippet of hope had evaporated. Ida had carried that snippet of hope ever since Christmas Day, holding onto the idea that someone would wake up and realize a terrible mistake had been made and then set everything right... that there might be a miracle, in spite of everything.

Ida had become somewhat notorious herself as the wife of a local outlaw. The whole township had seen her at the trial. There was no one in their community who did not know, who had not heard of William Dodson and the murdered peddler. After the trial, it was next to impossible for Ida to find anyone who would consider hiring an outlaw's wife to clean house or wash clothes. Her parents helped out as best they could, but they could only spare a few dollars. A few dollars didn't go far with seven mouths to feed.

The older children tried to contribute. Young Will was able to bring in some money by trapping skunks, skinning them with his father's pocketknife, and selling the pelts. Rhoda and Rebecca found odd jobs in neighboring towns, as long as they didn't give their real names. But what they brought in was meager at best. The job of putting food on the table increasingly fell to the older Dodson children. The family had their vegetable patch, and Will fished for trout in the Clarion River and trapped rabbit and pheasant. But time spent providing for essentials meant time not spent at his books, and this broke Will's heart.

As the weeks turned into months and the months into a year, Ida grew more distant from her children. Besides food, her children needed shoes and clothing. The house was falling into disrepair and she could no longer ask a friendly neighbor for help. Something inside her had broken, never to be mended. She cared for baby Jimmy as best she could, and then left him with Linnie and Gracie when she went off on those day-long searches for a job. Any job.

One day, Ida had traveled down to Reynoldsville, a good distance from home, in search of work. She saw a man sweeping his front porch and, forcing a pleasant smile, approached him.

"Pardon me, sir. I was wondering if you and your family needed housekeeping?"

The man looked her up and down in a way that made her feel

unclean.

"We don't need the likes of you around here." The man paused to run his hand up and down the broom. "Unless you'd be interested in…"

Ida hurried off down the street before the man could finish his disgusting proposal.

She returned to her home late that night, empty-handed.

"Mama!" Gracie was on the floor playing with little Jimmy. "Look, Mama, Jimmy almost spelled my name." She pointed to her Poppa's blocks.

"C – R – A – G – I – E," said Ida, her voice dull and distant. She looked at the blocks and then she looked at her two youngest children, and she couldn't for the life of her understand why her life had been destroyed or what she had done to deserve it.

The next day, Ida caught a ride with a traveling dry goods salesman who had business in Sykesville. The salesman tried to make conversation along the road, but Ida could only bring herself to answer in monosyllables. When they arrived at the edge of town, she jumped from his carriage and walked toward the first house she saw.

"Good morning," she said to the man who opened the front door. "I was wondering if I could find employment here."

"I know who you are," said the man, a sly look in his eye. "The only work I got for you… is this." He grabbed his crotch.

"Yeah? How much?" said Ida.

It was as though someone else had said the words. That first time was difficult, but not as difficult as watching her children go hungry. The man paid her more money than she would have made cleaning his house. Soon the scenario became routine. After a few weeks, Ida became adept at manipulation: first she would ask for legitimate work, and then lead her mark – even the most upstanding of men – into the inevitable lewd comment. Which led to the payoff. Sex for money.

It's for the children, she told herself.

It also became her escape from reality. In a short time, she realized she enjoyed the attention from random strangers. For that brief period of time, she felt important; she felt like somebody. Even if she had to sell her body, the feeling of power became addictive. When one of the three oldest children was home, Ida would take off for long periods of time. "Going out to get some supplies," she'd say.

Soon she was doing it every day.

Now the family's basic needs were met: there was food and clothing and even new leg braces for Gracie, who was growing fast. But what the children needed most – their mother's love and affection – Ida could no longer give.

The children all sensed their mother had changed, but did not know the real reason.

"She's mad about Pop," said Will. "I'm mad, too." He said it with an air of finality. He was through defending his father and had other things to think about – trying to keep up with his schoolwork *and* take care of all his siblings. With Ida no longer at home to keep order in the household, Will was boss. The children clung to him and to each other.

CHAPTER FOURTEEN

"I'm gonna be Mama today," said Gracie, as she pulled long socks on little brother Jimmy's feet.

"No, *I'm* gonna be Mama," said Linnie, as she stuffed Jimmy's arms into his sweater. Gracie glared at her sister.

"Okay, we can *both* be Mama," said Linnie.

Gracie smiled with satisfaction. "We give him breakfast now," she said. She tried to pick him up and carry him to the kitchen; Linnie watched her struggle and gently lifted the baby from her arms.

"That's right, Gracie. You can feed him."

Rhoda and Rebecca had made porridge before they went off to school that morning, and the lumpy grey mound in the bottom of the pot was still warm. Linnie spooned some into a bowl and handed it to Gracie.

"Here, Jimmy, eat," she said as she put a spoonful to his lips. Jimmy opened his mouth wide and then shut it tight before Gracie could get the stuff into his mouth.

"Oh, you're a bad boy," said Gracie. Linnie giggled.

Later on that day, after Rhoda and Rebecca had come home, there was a knock on the door.

Rhoda peeked through the curtain. "It's a priest!"

Father Winkler was the priest from the Church of the Immaculate Conception, the Catholic church in Brookville where the family had occasionally attended Sunday Mass.

"You'd better let him in," said Rebecca.

Rhoda opened the door. "Good afternoon, Father," she said.

"Good afternoon, children," said the priest. He stood on the threshold and looked around the front room. Linnie had the baby on her lap and Gracie was on the floor, trying to make her Poppa's blocks spin like little tops.

"May I come in?" asked Father Winkler.

Rhoda stepped back from the doorway.

"How are you children today?" said the Father.

"We're fine," said Rebecca.

"Where is your mother?"

"She went to run some errands," said Rhoda.

"I see," said the Father. He removed his spectacles, wiped them with a handkerchief, and put them back on his nose. "I'd like to talk to her, if I may."

The children looked at one another. No one said a word.

"Perhaps I should come back another time," suggested the Father.

"Yes," said Rhoda. "She may be back soon, or she may be back in a while."

Father Winkler began to make it a practice to stop in at the Dodson house every week or so. Rumors of neglect, that things were not as they should be, had reached the local authorities. The Father would vary the time of day of his visits, sometimes dropping by in the morning, sometimes in the late afternoon.

One afternoon, Will answered the door. *It's that darned priest again*, he thought to himself. *Why won't he leave us alone?*

Father Winkler didn't wait to be invited into the house; he just walked right in and looked around suspiciously.

"Can I help you, Father?" asked Will, trying to suppress his annoyance.

"Where is your mother, son?" asked the priest.

"She's working, I think she went to Sykesville," answered Will.

"Hmmm," said the priest.

But before the good Father could report his latest findings to the authorities, Ida Dodson was arrested for prostitution and adultery. To add insult to injury, she was also charged with child neglect. It had been two years since her husband was imprisoned for murder. The children didn't know why their mother hadn't come home from what they assumed was another long day looking for work in far-flung towns. They hadn't been particularly worried. Will had assured them their mother had probably missed her ride back.

On the morning following Ida's arrest, Father Winkler arrived at the Dodson home with a court order to remove the children. He had two nuns along with him. Will was already awake and dressed – he was always the first one up in the mornings and had started the fire in the stove. The other children were still in their nightclothes.

The loud pounding on the door made all the children jump.

"Children! Open up!" called Father Winkler from the porch. The two nuns stood behind him. "Open up!" he called, much louder. "We've come to take care of you."

Will's first instinct was to get himself and his siblings to a safe hiding place. But where? He stood petrified in the middle of the room. He turned to give the others a sign: *Keep quiet. Maybe they'll go away if they think we're not here.*

Rhoda and Rebecca huddled together at the window near the rear of the cabin. Gracie crouched in the corner, her eyes as big as saucers. Linnie ran to little Jimmy to keep him quiet.

"Come on now, open the door," called Father Winkler. "Will? We know you're in there. We're not going away, my son. Let us in."

Will was caught off guard. He tried to think. *If we all ran out the back, where would we go? We have no place to go.*

For an instant he thought about making a break alone, but he knew he could never leave his family behind. Not when they needed him more than ever.

"Just break the door down," said the older of the two nuns.

"Have some mercy, Sister Mary, and a little patience," said Father Winkler. "They'll open the door."

Will remembered Father Winkler from when the family used to attend Mass. He remembered liking his voice – a strong, comforting voice in the church. But Will had run out of options. He couldn't run by himself and he couldn't figure out a mass escape for his entire family. He reluctantly slid open the latch on the door.

CHAPTER FIFTEEN

When he heard the latch lift from its slot, Father Winkler lunged at the door and burst into the cabin, almost knocking Will to the floor. The back window slammed shut, but no one heard it over little Jimmy's screaming. Linnie sat on the floor, holding him tight, rocking back and forth. Gracie was still hunched down in the corner, too frightened to even cry.

"What do you want?" said Will. "You'll wake up our Mama."

"Your mother's not here, child," said the older nun, grabbing hold of his shirt. "She's in jail where she belongs."

"What do you mean, she's in jail?" shouted Will. "For what?"

"Your mother's a whore. A common street-walker. God have mercy on her soul." Will looked at the nun's fat fist still clutching his shirt and then into her face; her eyes were small and mean. He tried to shake her off.

"Enough, Sister," said Father Winkler. "Have you no sympathy for these poor innocent children? They have been through enough. Now let's get them cleaned up and dressed and be on our way."

Baby Jimmy was still screaming and Gracie had squeezed herself into the corner, trying to make herself small enough to disappear.

"We're not going anywhere with you," said Will, trying to stand his ground while the nun yanked on his shirt.

"Sister Mary, let go of him!" demanded the priest. The nun shoved Will back in disgust.

"We're taking you to a better place," said Father Winkler, keeping his voice calm, as he tried in vain to ease the escalating chaos. But Sister Mary had no interest in keeping anyone calm, nor did she seem to have any idea how to talk to frightened children.

"Will you quiet that screaming orphan?" she yelled at the younger nun, who rushed over and snatched Jimmy from Linnie's arms. The girl struggled to hold on to her little brother and his screams rose to a shattering pitch. Sister Mary closed her eyes and ground her teeth for a moment. Then she spun around. "Where are your sisters?"

Will spun around, too. *They were right here*, he thought to himself. Father Winkler made a slow circle to check every corner of the room. "Go look upstairs," he instructed the younger nun. For the first time, everyone noticed the back window slamming against its frame in the morning breeze.

Rhoda and Rebecca had escaped.

"How am I going to explain the two that got away?" Father Winkler mumbled to the nuns.

Being a middle-level functionary in his church, Father Winkler was burdened with the fears and concerns of middle management; he would have to answer not only to the diocese but also to the local authorities.

"They'll be found," replied Sister Mary. "I'm sure they won't get far."

While the younger nun tended to little Jimmy, short-tempered Sister Mary dealt with Linnie and Gracie. She told them to wash themselves and when the girls didn't comply, she grabbed them and scrubbed them with cold water like they were a pair of dirty dishes. Then she brushed their hair, hard, every stroke yanking at their tender scalps.

Sister Mary found clothes in a cedar chest and tried to pull and prod the girls into their dresses.

"Those are our Sunday clothes," Linnie protested. "It's *not* Sunday!"

The nun responded by slapping her across the face. "Don't you talk back to me, little girl. Now hush that mouth of yours and put these on."

Linnie started to wail.

"Don't you dare cry or I'll slap you again."

Gracie just watched, too scared to move. She did not want to get slapped.

"That means you, too!" Sister Mary shouted at Gracie. "Get dressed!"

The girls reluctantly put on their Sunday clothes: matching heavy woolen, high-collared plaid dresses.

Father Winkler told Will to change his shirt and empty his pockets. The only possession the boy had was his father's pocketknife and now he always carried it with him. He even slept with it under his pillow. Father Winkler took it away. More than ever, Will wished they had all tried to make a run for it, like Rhoda and Rebecca. He prayed his two sisters would not be caught.

"You children won't be taking anything with you. Just the clothes you are wearing," said Father Winkler."

"Yes," chimed in Sister Mary. "Where you're going, you won't need anything from this filthy place."

When the nuns weren't looking, Gracie stuffed her precious blocks into the pockets of her dress.

"What's that in your pockets, child?" barked Sister Mary.

Gracie stood at attention, her arms at her sides. With one hand the nun held the little girl firmly by the shoulder so that she couldn't move, and with the other reached into the bulging pockets. One by one, she pulled out the six wooden blocks and flung them across the room like trash. Gracie remained frozen in place, afraid of getting slapped like her sister. She simply glared at Sister Mary with more hatred than she had ever felt toward another human being.

Linnie screamed at the nun for being so nasty to her little sister. Sister Mary, determined to slap some manners into this devil-child, went after her again with a vengeance. But while the mean nun was going after Linnie and the young nun was upstairs dressing little Jimmy, Gracie quickly gathered up the blocks and cradled them in the skirt of her dress. She carried them to a loose floorboard near the stove. It was a secret hiding place only she knew about. Swiftly, she lifted the loosened board and placed each of her Poppa's blocks into the hole. "You'll be safe in here," she whispered, "'till I get back for you."

Just as Gracie slid the board back into place, Sister Mary pulled Linnie into the room by her ponytail. With her free hand, the nun grabbed Gracie by the arm and jerked them both to the front door. The younger nun carried little Jimmy down the stairs. He was dressed in a long-sleeved cotton shirt with sailor collar and cuffs, a sailor tie, and the plaid pleated skirt that had belonged to Will when he was little. It was customary at the time to dress infant boys in skirts, graduating to short trousers and finally to long pants.

Father Winkler and Will were already waiting in an open horse-drawn wagon that looked like it had been built in a pre-Civil War wagonworks.

"Where's Gracie's braces?" said Will.

Father Winkler's eyes shot from Gracie's legs to the eyes of Sister Mary. "Go get her braces," he ordered, knowing the sister had deliberately left them behind.

Sister Mary lumbered back up the steps to the cabin. "Nobody's going to want to adopt a child that looks crippled," she muttered to herself.

She found the braces and brought them back to the wagon.

"Now put them on the child," commanded Father Winkler.

"No, I'll do it!" cried Will. He knew the chances of Sister Mary getting leg braces on Gracie were slim to none.

CHAPTER SIXTEEN

The old wagon bumped along the country road, every jolt a rude reminder that the Dodson children's lives would never be the same. Will stared straight ahead, stone-faced. Father Winkler tried at first to make conversation but gave up after his questions about Will's school studies were answered with noncommittal grunts. Gracie and Linnie, sandwiched between Sister Mary and the younger nun, Sister Josephine, clutched each other's hands and stole fearful glances at each other. There were tears in Linnie's eyes but Gracie willed herself not to cry.

About a mile into the journey, Sister Josephine pulled several rosaries from the deep pockets of her habit. Each was a different color. She handed a rosary to each child and tucked one into the pocket of Jimmy's skirt.

"That's all you'll need from now on," said Sister Mary. "You do know how to pray the rosary, don't you?"

The children stared at the string of beads in their hands and said nothing. None of them had seen a rosary before.

"Jesus, Mary and Joseph! Just put them in your pockets!" said the exasperated nun. "You'll need them where you're going."

Father Winkler turned around and glared at her angrily. "It is not the children's fault they've received no religious instruction," he said in a grim voice.

Grace was fascinated by the beads. She held them between her fingers and examined their smooth roundness; then she tried to put the rosary around her neck. Sister Josephine smacked Gracie's hands.

"No! You do *not* wear your rosary like a necklace!"

Tears sprang to Gracie's eyes as she put the beads in the pocket of her dress.

Father Winkler turned off the country lane onto the main road that led into town.

Why are we going to Brookville? Will wondered. *Maybe Father Winkler is going to take us to school.*

That would have been all right. Instead, the priest stopped the wagon in front of the jailhouse.

"Come, children."

Father Winkler lifted Gracie out of the wagon first. Her eyes grew big as saucers when she saw the bars on the windows. Linnie started to whimper but Gracie put her finger to her lips and gave her older sister a warning glance. Will climbed out of the wagon and looked up and down the street. He saw nobody he knew, no one he could ask for help.

The priest clamped a hand on Will's shoulder and told him to carry his baby brother. Then he told Linnie to take her little sister's hand. "There is someone who wants to see you," said Father Winkler.

He marched the Dodson children into the jailhouse and down a long corridor. They passed a cell where they saw an old man asleep on the floor. His skin was encrusted with dirt and his clothes looked like rags. The children huddled together as Father Winkler herded them deeper into the jail.

Suddenly, the children froze. In the next cell, on the other side of the bars, was Ida Dodson. She was sitting on a dirty mattress; her dress was soiled and her hair was long and uncombed.

"Go on, children," said Father Winkler, coaxing them closer to the bars. "I thought you would like to say a word or two to your mother."

But the children did not budge. Ida jumped up from her mattress and came as close to her children as the bars would permit. She looked into their faces, but they looked back at her in horror.

"Go on!" repeated Father Winkler, unable to suppress his annoyance. "At least say goodbye." But the children stood frozen in place. Not a word was spoken by any of them.

How could she have allowed this to happen? We were getting along fine without you. We were taking care of each other. Why?

Not even little Jimmy wanted his mother. Ida simply stared back at her children, as if searching each pair of eyes for a glimmer of forgiveness. There was none to be found. Tears trickled down her cheeks. There was no love left in the hearts of her children. She had abandoned them.

"Fine!" blurted Father Winkler. "We're going now. It's a long way to Erie. Good luck, Ida. Say goodbye to the State's newest orphans!"

He herded the children down the corridor and out of the jailhouse. Unable to utter a sound, Ida collapsed on the mattress, tears of shame, remorse and inconceivable loss running down her face. She would never earn her children's forgiveness and she knew she would never be able to forgive herself.

It was the last time Ida ever saw any of her children. She was tried and found guilty on all counts – adultery, prostitution and child neglect. And like her husband, she was sentenced to serve time behind bars.

It was the spring of 1899. The Dodson children never mentioned their mother's existence ever again. From that day forward, silence would become their weapon and companion. The less said, the less they would have to be sorry about.

The wagon trip to Erie took almost seven hours. Nobody spoke, not even Sister Mary. As evening fell, their new home suddenly loomed, dark and sinister, before the frightened children. Silhouetted against the setting sun stood the largest structure they'd ever seen, two medieval-looking towers flanking a high-pitched roof with a huge cross on top. The cross cast eerie shadows on the ground.

"Bless you, my children," said Father Winkler. "You'll be better off now." The children looked at him with questions in their eyes. Sister Mary was already on the ground as Sister Josephine climbed down from the wagon with baby Jimmy in her arms.

"Come, come, children!" said Sister Mary, clapping her hands loudly. "Out!"

In the short time the children had spent with Father Winkler, they had come to realize that he was their only protector; he seemed to have their best interests at heart. But he would not be joining them in this place. The nuns herded the children up to the massive front doors of St. Joseph's Orphan Home. Will turned around to look at Father Winkler.

The priest gave him an encouraging nod. "You'll be better off, my boy," he called, as if he'd read Will's mind.

"We'll be in touch, Father," Sister Mary yelled, as she pushed the children through the huge wooden doors... like lambs to the slaughter.

CHAPTER SEVENTEEN

The doors slammed shut behind the Dodson children with a terrifying thud that echoed through the building, a signal to all inside that new inmates had arrived. It dawned on them that they were now alone, at the mercy of Sister Mary and Sister Josephine, who were now on their own turf. Without Father Winkler's calming influence, Sister Mary could give her natural bad temper and brutality free reign.

"You watch those girls!" she snapped at Sister Josephine as she gave Will a rude shove. The frightened children were pushed through the church to a dark hallway and a closed door. Josephine handed little Jimmy to his older brother.

Sister Mary rapped loudly on the door before she pushed it open.

"Mother Eugenia, these are the newest arrivals."

The Mother Superior was seated behind a large desk in a small, starkly furnished office. The head of St. Joseph's Orphanage and the person to whom all the sisters reported was in her late sixties. There was no softness in her face. Mother Eugenia was the boss. She removed her glasses and stood up to inspect the new arrivals huddled together before her. Like the other sisters, she was dressed in a black and white habit. Wrapped around her waist was a heavy sash made of rope tied with three large knots at each end.

She peered at Will who cradled Jimmy in his arms. "How old is he?"

"Two and a half," Will replied, with all the courage he could muster.

"And you?"

Will didn't answer. He just stood there, defiant, tightening his hold on his little brother.

The Mother Superior repeated the question, articulating each word loudly and sharply as if she were speaking to a deaf person. "And *you*? How old are you?"

She glared at Will and all the children glared back at her. But Will could not win this standoff. "Fourteen," he answered.

"Sister Josephine," the Mother Superior barked, "please take that child to the infant ward." She kept her eyes glued to Will's, as if to test him.

Sister Josephine reached for little Jimmy, but Will tightened his grip on his little brother and jerked clear of her grasp. "No!" he shouted. "He stays with us."

"No, he doesn't," said Sister Josephine as she grabbed Jimmy from Will's arms. Jimmy started to cry, which set off Linnie and Gracie, and soon the small room was filled with crying children.

"Sister Mary!" yelled the Mother Superior, massaging her temples with her fingertips. "I am not going to deal with insolent children at this late hour. Take the girls, clean them up and put them to bed without supper. They will learn not to behave like heathens in my presence."

Sister Mary grabbed Linnie and Gracie by their arms and jerked them away from their big brother. Will, their protector and caregiver, was not going to give them up without a fight; he reached out for his sisters. As he tried to pull them away from Sister Mary, a loud, sharp crack reverberated through Mother Eugenia's office. Will's hand jolted open and a sharp pain shot through his entire body; the right side of his face turned bright red as a huge welt rose up on his cheek. Mother Superior stood ready to deliver a second blow from the heavy knotted rope around her waist.

That was the last time Linnie and Gracie saw their older brother. The horrible scene in Mother Superior's office, Will standing there stunned, confused and hurt with an angry welt growing on his cheek, was the last image the sisters had of their protector. The next morning, just before dawn, he was transported to Father Baker's Home for Boys in Buffalo, New York. He had no opportunity to say goodbye to what was left of his family.

Grace and her siblings had been brought to St. Joseph's "for their own protection" – or so they'd been told. "For a better life." They weren't even orphans. But an orphan asylum was not a healthy place for children, particularly around the turn of the last century. The St. Joseph's Orphan's Home was part of St. Patrick's Church, the first Catholic Church in Erie. Economic conditions had left a staggering number of children homeless. Many who resided in orphan asylums were not technically orphans; these children had a mother or a father or both parents, but the parents were unable to care for them and saw the asylums as their only solution. From 1899 to 1903, the number of orphaned children at various institutions soared to unimaginable and unmanageable levels. Most of these institutions found themselves trying to feed and care for a population far beyond their means and capacity. St. Joseph's was no exception.

What happened to the Dodson children was replicated in homes throughout the country in the late 1890s. Families grew and events overtook them. Fathers might lose a job, or become injured and unable to work or, worse, lose their lives; their wives and children were left without means of support.

Gracie and her siblings had not become wards of the state because of a single stroke of economic bad luck. They were victims of a series of circumstances completely beyond their control.

The children's bad luck would continue.

In order to manage an ever-increasing number of inmates, the routine at St. Joseph's and orphanages like it had to be highly regimented. Children were herded together in large groups, marched out of their dormitories at the crack of dawn for early morning Mass. Then they were marched to a drafty dining hall for a breakfast of barely edible porridge, followed by chores, school work and catechism class. After that, they were marched back for a dinner of boiled meat and potatoes, then evening prayers and finally to bed.

After a life of relative freedom, particularly in the two years between their father's conviction and their mother's arrest, when Ida was seldom at home, the children were unaccustomed to such strict regimentation. They were also unaccustomed to having to remain indoors so much of the time, and to being told what to do and when to do it by nuns whose faces were as severe as their habits.

"Get back into line, you!" shouted a nun and she smacked Linnie on her bottom as the children were waiting to enter the dining hall. Gracie was standing farther back in line, but close enough to see and hear her sister's humiliation. She burned in anger but kept silent and made sure she was standing directly behind the child in front of her.

A week after their arrival at the orphanage, Mother Superior received a letter from Father Winkler confirming the Dodson children's forthcoming legal status, along with a meager check to help defray expenses:

March 21, 1899
Church of Immaculate Conception
Brookville, PA

Dear Mother Eugenia,
Enclosed please find a $100 check. This is all the money I could get from the commissioners. I am having the papers made out and as soon as they are ready, I will send them to the father (in prison) to have them signed. The lawyers here informed me that would be of more value than the signature of the commissioners.
Wishing you the blessings of the season.

I am sincerely yours,
FA. Geo. Winkler

Mother Eugenia read the letter and called Sister Josephine into her office.

"Please remove the Dodson girl's braces," she told the nun. "And discard them. No one wants to adopt a crippled child, or a child who looks crippled."

Sister Josephine nodded curtly and left the office. Then Mother Eugenia found Grace's paperwork and added a year to her age. This would make her more desirable for adoption. In those days, most families seeking to adopt or provide a temporary foster home to children from orphanages were simply looking for manual laborers or domestic help they didn't have to pay for. It was rare that someone wanted to provide a loving home to an orphaned child. Strong, healthy children were chosen first.

A month later, the formal documents relinquishing all parental rights arrived on Mother Superior's desk, duly signed by William Dodson. The children were now officially and legally wards of the State and eligible for adoption.

CHAPTER EIGHTEEN

First they had to be baptized. Evidently, Mother Superior did not believe that orphans merited a traditional baptism in St. Joseph's church. Instead, the ceremony was performed in the classroom and it took all of two minutes. Grace Caroline Dodson was christened Mary Josephine. Melinda Jane – Linnie – was christened Mary Teresa, and little Jesse James was christened James Joseph. At least he got to keep one of his real names. The children were instructed never to use their original names again under threat of the rod or rope or worse. The Catholics believed that if the children were given the name of a saint, that saint would serve as their special patron and watch over, guide and protect them. Gracie would not have minded being named after saints, but not after the two nuns she hated the most. It was a name she would never accept.

Overcrowded and understaffed, St. Joseph's operated like a poorly outfitted factory with the purpose of feeding, housing and educating children until they could be adopted. The children were a kind of product pushed through the assembly line, or more accurately, an endless series of lines. While the occasional newspaper article portrayed orphanages as safe dwellings where happy, rosy-cheeked children played, went to school and learned Christian conduct, the reality was quite different. Many children were malnourished because

87

there often wasn't enough food to go around, and what was there, was badly cooked. Good medical care was almost nonexistent. The younger ones, most of whom, like the Dodsons, had one or both parents still alive, carried false hope that their parents would one day return for them. Many of the older children looked forward to the chance of being adopted... trading the hell they knew for an unknown hell.

There was a strict rule that no child was allowed out of bed after the lights were turned out – not even to use the bathroom. Every night, one of the nuns would patrol the dorm rooms; heaven help the child who was not in his or her own bed.

During the first few months after Gracie came to St. Joseph's, she found it impossible to go to sleep without seeing her sister Linnie. The Mother Superior had separated the girls, a common practice with siblings, and placed them in different dorm rooms. Despite many warnings, Gracie risked punishment: every night after lights-out, she would sneak into Linnie's dorm room. She would count down the long row of beds to number twelve, her sister's bed, and stay just long enough to say good night. Then she would slip back to her own bed and fall asleep, satisfied that her only remaining sister was safe.

Gracie had been caught once or twice and soundly spanked, but punishment didn't stop her from seeing her sister the only time and place she could. The girls never saw each other in class or at mealtimes; the nuns made sure of that. The prevailing theory was that siblings should be separated early to ease the inevitable pain that will come when one is adopted and the other is left behind. But this tactic had the opposite effect: the sisters tried even harder to sneak around and find each other, any way they could.

One night Gracie managed to get to Linnie's dorm room but could not rouse her from her deep sleep. "Linnie?" she whispered and gave her sister a little shake. "Wake up, it's me."

Linnie rolled over and Gracie climbed into bed alongside her. She planned to stay only a couple of minutes, but instead fell sound asleep.

Then all hell broke loose.

Gracie found herself on the floor, screaming, silver spots floating in front of her eyes from an agonizing pain in the side of her head. The nun on patrol had found her asleep with Linnie, grabbed hold of Gracie's long blonde hair and yanked her out of bed. As Gracie lay sprawled, screaming on the cold, stone floor and Linnie began to cry hysterically, the nun realized she was holding a hank of Gracie's hair in her fist. All the other little girls were awake now, sitting up in bed and looking open-mouthed from Gracie clutching the side of her head to the nun standing frozen with Gracie's hair entwined in her fingers.

The nun snapped into action when she realized everyone was staring at her, and lunged for Gracie as the little girl kicked and screamed and tried to get away. But Gracie was too little and not fast enough. The nun grabbed her by her foot and dragged her on her back through the dorm, past each bed, past every horrified child. When they reached the hall, the nun slammed the door behind them. The children heard Gracie's screams echoing down the hall and then... silence.

At the end of the hall, under the staircase, was a small, dark closet where Gracie spent the rest of that night. The nun locked the door and left her to cry until dawn. Her tears ebbed and flowed, and when her little body, exhausted from emotion, started to take her toward slumber, she reached up and felt the blood congealing in her scalp where the nun had ripped out her hair. She thought about Linnie and wondered why they could not be together, and her tears and sobs began all over again.

The next morning, a different nun unlocked the closet and brought Gracie into an empty classroom. Gracie was sure she was in for more punishment.

"Sit down, child," said the nun. Her voice was soft and kind. Gracie looked up at the nun suspiciously, unwilling to take a seat.

"Go on, Mary Josephine. It's all right. We're going to fix your hair."

The nun took a washcloth and dipped it in a basin of cool water. "My name is Sister Margaret Elizabeth."

Sister Margaret gently washed Gracie's raw scalp. Gracie winced.

"There, there. All done." Then the nun took a pair of scissors and cut off what remained of Gracie's long, golden locks. As she clipped, Sister Margaret stood back to study her work. Gracie's heart was pounding but she did not say a word.

When the nun had finished, Gracie had a very short, slightly lopsided haircut.

Punishment can be loud and punishment can be quiet, too, she said to herself.

From that day on, she never ventured from her bed again after lights out.

CHAPTER NINETEEN

Soon Gracie no longer had reason to go looking for her sister; a week after the haircut, Linnie left the orphanage.

It was a Saturday morning, and like every Saturday morning at St. Joseph's, the nuns made the orphans line up for visitor inspection. Mother Eugenia would escort the visitors down the line, inspecting the children as if they were cattle on an auction block. It was just one more in the endless series of ordeals of living at St. Joseph's. Linnie still liked to hide, especially before visitor inspections. But on this day, Sister Ignatia found her crouched under the staircase. With a grip of steel, the sister marched Linnie to the end of the line-up and released her with a deliberate jerk. The visitor on this particular Saturday was a large man in a brown tweed coat. He was interested in adopting a female, therefore only the girls had been rounded up.

Gracie watched from her place in the line as the gentleman walked slowly down the row of girls, with Mother Eugenia a few deferential steps behind him. He paused briefly to evaluate each one but he barely glanced at Gracie. He had already been to three orphanages that morning and was about to give up for the day, when he came to Linnie at the end of the line.

Linnie kept her head bowed and stared at the floor. She did not want to look the man in the eye, afraid she might be chosen. More than anything, she didn't want to leave her sister and little Jimmy behind.

"What's your name?" he asked. Linnie stared resolutely at the floor and did not respond.

"Does she speak? Is she mute? Or is she retarded?" asked the man as he turned impatiently toward Mother Eugenia, expecting a quick answer.

"Yes, she speaks just fine. And no, she is not retarded. In fact, she is one of the smartest and strongest we have," replied Mother Eugenia. She would have said that of any child he'd asked about. "Her name is Mary Teresa."

The man softened his posture and bent toward Linnie. "How old are you, Mary Teresa?" He tried to sound polite, remembering he was speaking to a little girl who had lost her parents. But Linnie still didn't answer and kept her head bowed.

Mother Eugenia's eyes flashed in anger. She extended her index finger and firmly lifted Linnie's chin, forcing her to look directly at the gentleman's face. "Answer him," she demanded, using her sweetest voice.

"My name is Linnie," she said defiantly. "And I am seven."

The Mother Superior's blood boiled. It was all she could do not to slap this insolent child across the face. But the gentleman nodded and smiled, amused by the child's show of spirit. "Linnie, is it? Can you open your mouth for me, Linnie?"

Linnie just looked at him. The man was running out of patience. He took hold of her cheeks and squeezed hard. "Open!" he demanded.

Linnie squirmed but reluctantly opened her mouth for his inspection. The last thing the man wanted was a sickly child who would cost him money for doctor's bills.

Suddenly Gracie jumped out of line and ran awkwardly – as fast as her bowed legs would take her – toward her sister. "Leave her alone!"

Sister Ignatia leaped into Gracie's path and grabbed her by the arm. "Sorry, sir, they're sisters," said the nun.

"Linnie! Linnie!" Gracie screamed, as Sister Ignatia carried her from the room.

"Pity," said the man. "I might have taken them both. What happened to her hair?"

"Head lice," answered Mother Eugenia. "We had to cut it."

The next morning, Gracie raced through the orphanage looking for her sister, hoping against hope that the large man hadn't taken her away. She scanned the girls in the dining room, in the classrooms, in morning chapel; she ran outside. Linnie was nowhere to be found. It was Sister Margaret who found Gracie leaning against the brick wall by the scrubby dirt field with a few blades of grass that Mother Superior optimistically called a playground.

"Your sister's gone, child," said the nun. "She's been adopted by that nice gentleman who visited yesterday."

Gracie's heart sank. But she made up her mind she would not cry in front of Sister Margaret. She would try her best not to cry in front of any of the nuns from now on. More than ever, she was determined to stay as close as she could to Jimmy, the only brother she had left. Even if it meant severe punishment.

The girls' section of the orphanage was separated from the boys' and seldom was there any interaction between the two. Between the boys' and girls' dormitories was the playground, divided by a tall chain-link fence. The girls played on one side, the boys on the other. Gracie had not seen much of her little brother for the past few months, and Linnie's disappearance only made her more compelled to see him. Instead of using the scant forty-five minutes allocated for playing, Gracie would spend her whole recess standing at the fence, searching the faces of the little boys on the other side. One afternoon she finally spotted him.

"Jimmy!"

Her little brother came running to the fence. They grinned at each other and stuck their hands through the chain-link. Jimmy was growing into a sturdy little boy; Gracie held his little hand in hers and studied his chubby fingers. She wondered if the nuns on the other side fed the boys better than they fed the girls.

Every afternoon thereafter, Gracie and Jimmy would meet at the fence, just for a few moments. They knew they had to be careful not to let the nuns see them. But their routine lasted only a few weeks. Another little girl, jealous that Gracie had a family member "inside," told the nuns about the forbidden rendezvous, and Gracie was warned to stay away from the fence.

But neither threats nor punishment would stop her. When spankings failed, the nuns brought Gracie to the Mother Superior's office. Gracie planted herself firmly on her little bowed legs as Mother Eugenia rose from behind her desk. The woman was accustomed to using the power of her grim presence, her whip hand and sharp voice, and all the orphans lived in fear of crossing her. She could not understand why this child was so hard to manage. The little girl just glared at her, chin raised, eyes defiant.

This was too much.

Swiftly, Mother Eugenia moved around her desk and boxed the child on both ears.

The blows landed hard, but worse than the pain was the sudden loss of hearing. Gracie went stone deaf for a few seconds. She stood there stunned, her mouth open. She did not cry. Instead she began to work her jaw until she felt something pop, first in her left ear, then the right.

"Mary Josephine," said the Mother Superior. Gracie stared hard at the woman. "You have displayed nothing but defiance and disregard of our rules since you arrived at St. Joseph's."

The Mother Superior's voice was growing louder. Gracie cautiously rubbed one ear.

"You *will* obey, child," she said, as she fingered the knotted belt around her waist. "And you will stay away from the fence."

CHAPTER TWENTY

But Gracie couldn't stay away from the fence. The more the nuns whipped her, the stronger her resolve to see her brother became. Not even Mother Eugenia's knotted rope could change her mind. Finally the nuns were forced to rearrange the playground schedule, so that the girls never saw the boys across the dirt field. Gracie was heartbroken; now she would never get to see her little brother. But at the same time she felt something new growing within her: a sense of power in the face of impossible and devastating circumstances. She had learned to steel herself through all the beatings, willed herself not to cry out, not to give the nuns the satisfaction of knowing that they'd hurt her.

Six months later Jimmy was adopted. However, Mother Eugenia thought it best to tell Gracie that her little brother had died.

"It will be easier for Mary Josephine to accept the fact that her brother is dead," the Mother Superior decreed, "than for her to hold on to some vain hope he may come back." Such was the prevailing wisdom of St. Joseph's Home for Children. One of the other sisters took Gracie aside.

"Jimmy is dead," said the nun. She didn't look Gracie in the eye when she spoke.

"What?

The sister kept her eyes averted. "Your little brother Jimmy is dead."

The pain in the little girl's heart was almost unbearable. She bit her lip and tried to stop the tears that filled her eyes and threatened to spill onto her cheeks. Turning her face away from the nun, Gracie asked to be excused.

Soon thereafter, a letter from Father Baker's Home in New York arrived at the orphanage. It was addressed to the Dodson Children. The Mother Superior opened the envelope, but it contained no letter, no note, just a single string of rosary beads. She knew immediately what it meant and had one of the nuns take the rosary to Gracie, the only Dodson still at the asylum. The nun did not have to explain: Gracie knew instantly her brother Will had not survived. He had died at Father Baker's Home for Boys just a year after he arrived. He was only fifteen years old.

The most likely cause of death was tuberculosis, a disease that would not be brought under control for another fifty years. The bacterium spread quickly among people who were malnourished and living at close quarters; only the very wealthy could afford the few, often unsuccessful treatment options. Children and young adults were the biggest casualties. It was a sad ending for Will Dodson, the boy who was so determined to amount to something one day.

From that day forward, Gracie made it through each day's routine, but with never a laugh, not even a smile. She had learned to cry in silence. The adorable child with the angelic face and enormous zest for life was gone, replaced by an automaton who did what she was told and followed the rules at the orphanage. There was no longer any reason to break them. Everyone she had ever loved had been taken from her, one by one.

While Gracie had had one or two friends at St. Joseph's, she had learned it was better not to form strong attachments; the people you loved most would leave or be taken away from you. She made it a point to be cordial, but not too friendly with the other girls. The pain of so many losses in such a short time had hardened her shell and she became expert at keeping a blank mask upon her face.

An obedient child devoid of personality was a valuable commodity, one which St. Joseph's assembly line was proud to produce. Soon Gracie was picked out of the line-up for potential adoption. It was 1902 and she had just turned nine years old. An older gentleman with a rather young wife arrived on visitors' day and declared little Mary Josephine was exactly the sort of child they were looking for. They told the Mother Superior that they already had three children of their own, one of whom was a toddler who needed extra attention.

"Mary Josephine is a fine, obedient young lady," beamed the Mother Superior, speaking loudly and distinctly as if to reinforce her pronouncement upon Gracie.

"Would you like to come live with us?" asked the young wife.

"Yes, ma'am," said Gracie. She found she could not quite form her mouth into a smile but tried to sound sincere.

"Very well," said the gentleman. "It's settled."

Mr. and Mrs. Cotter and their three children lived in a large house in a well-to-do section of Erie. Gracie was shown to her room – little more than an alcove on the third floor furnished with a narrow bed and small chest of drawers – and she allowed herself a small, inward smile. The notion of sleeping by herself, of not having to sleep in an endless row of beds and children and not being subject to midnight nun patrol, made her feel as if perhaps life was finally taking a turn for the better.

"Is it all right, dear?" asked Mrs. Cotter.

"Yes, ma'am," said Gracie. "It's just fine."

"Good. Now I want you to meet the rest of the family." She took Gracie by the hand and led her downstairs to a large playroom on the second floor. Grace's mouth dropped open when she saw the toys scattered around the room: a huge doll with a shiny pink head that looked as if it were made out of china sat on a cushion, almost like a real child, and toy soldiers, dozens of them, lay scattered about the floor, amidst rubber balls of different colors. Over in a corner stood a rocking-horse, intricately carved and painted with bright-colored scrolls and flourishes along its sides. She drew in her breath and stared at this thing that was more work of art than toy; it reminded her of her Poppa's blocks.

"Who's she?"

The voice came from a boy who was reading in a corner of the room. He looked about twelve years old.

"That's not a polite thing to say, Peter. Say hello to Mary Josephine. She's from the orphanage," said Mrs. Cotter.

Peter peered over his reading glasses at Gracie with an expression that hovered between distaste and curiosity.

"Johnny! They did it!" Peter called into the next room. "They've brought us an orphan!"

Another boy bounded into the room. He appeared to be

almost the same age as Peter, perhaps a bit younger.

"Hah!" said Johnny. He ran over to the toy soldiers, gathered them up protectively, and put them in a large wooden box.

Mrs. Cotter seemed embarrassed. "Come, Mary Josephine. Let me show you the baby."

"Keep your hands off my toys, Mary Josephine," said Johnny as Mrs. Cotter led Gracie from the room.

Gracie kept her eyes straight ahead as Mrs. Cotter took her to the nursery. "This is our daughter, Genevieve. She's two and a half." A sturdy toddler with curly brown hair was standing up in her crib. When she saw her mother, she squealed and flailed her arms, and fell backward, landing on her bottom. Mrs. Cotter reached into the crib, picked up her daughter and held the little girl out to Gracie.

Gracie instinctively reached out to take the baby, but Mrs. Cotter wasn't quite ready to hand Genevieve over. Instead, she cuddled the baby in her arms, rocking her gently.

"She's awful pretty," said Gracie in a soft voice, thinking about how her father used to cuddle her in his arms, and how her brother Will had carried her everywhere when she was close to Genevieve's age. She felt a lump in her throat remembering the loving family she once had.

"Thank you. Yes, she is a very pretty baby."

"You all must love her an awful lot," said Gracie.

Mrs. Cotter's face clouded. She sat down in an armchair and cradled Genevieve in her lap. "Peter and Johnny are her half-brothers. Their mother passed away three years ago. I'm Mr. Cotter's second wife. It's been... difficult."

CHAPTER TWENTY-ONE

Gracie liked Mrs. Cotter. That first night, the lady of the house came into the kitchen to make sure the family's cook had given the new arrival enough to eat. While Mr. and Mrs. Cotter and the boys had their supper in the dining room, Gracie, the cook and Genevieve took their meal in the kitchen. The food was good and there was plenty of it – roast chicken, mashed potatoes and cornbread muffins.

But after a few days, Gracie began to feel almost sorry for Mrs. Cotter. The woman seemed as if she were trying to please everyone and ended up pleasing no one. She had absolutely no sway over her stepsons; the boys knew they could run roughshod over her and the house, and when she threatened to go to their father to punish them, they just sneered. When she did tell Mr. Cotter of his sons' bad behavior, he complained that she was not taking a firm enough hand with the boys.

Gracie's position in the house was that of nursemaid and babysitter. She was to attend to Genevieve when Mrs. Cotter went out and keep the nursery and its adjacent bathroom clean. She was also to help the cook at mealtimes. Gracie didn't mind her duties; in fact, she liked feeling useful and having tasks to perform every day. What she did not like was Peter and Johnny. They were always looking at her strangely, or whispering as soon as she left the room.

Years of living at the orphan asylum had taught Gracie a thing or two about how to sneak around unnoticed. One afternoon, after she'd put Genevieve down for her nap, she tiptoed down the hall and stationed herself just outside the boys' playroom.

"It's bad enough he married that woman," said Peter.

"And that woman had that baby," added Johnny.

"And now he's got some orphan taking care of the baby." Peter pronounced the word "orphan" as if it was a dirty word. "We don't know anything about her, or who her people were," he continued in his most superior tone. "For all we know, they could be criminals."

Gracie felt her face go red. In a flash, she was in the playroom and before she even realized what she was doing, she'd picked up the box of wooden soldiers and flung it as hard as she could. Little Prussians and Hessians and warriors from the Ottoman Empire lay scattered across the floor.

The next day she was returned to St. Joseph's. Mr. Cotter drove her himself in his fine carriage. He did not speak a word until they stopped in front of the ominous front doors to the orphanage. As he helped Gracie descend the steep carriage stairs, he told her, "Watch your step."

He marched ahead of her and pounded on the door.

"Well, what have we here?" said Sister Ignatia, peering down suspiciously at Gracie. Then, as if she suddenly remembered her manners, she murmured, "Good morning, Mr. Cotter. Please come in."

"I wish to speak to the Mother Superior," said Mr. Cotter.

"Alone."

Sister Ignatia understood what had happened. Little Mary Josephine had not proved to be a successful foster child. She grabbed Gracie roughly by the arm and hustled her into an empty classroom, slamming the door behind her.

Remolding her face into a fair imitation of piety and using her politest tone of voice, Sister Ignatia asked Mr. Cotter to follow her to Mother Eugenia's office.

Gracie heard their footsteps echoing down the hall. She wondered what sort of punishment she'd receive. She knew Mr. Cotter was angry with her; she knew it had been a bad idea to throw his sons' toys all over their room. But at least Mr. Cotter didn't display his anger. The Mother Superior would.

Discipline at St. Joseph's was at the discretion, or whim, of the clergy: being forced to kneel on a rock-hard floor for several excruciating hours to pray for forgiveness; or being slapped with a ruler across your open palm; or being slapped across the face so hard you thought your neck would snap. Or having your head shaved in front of the other children, *shaved into the shape of the cross.* The boys had it even worse: they were told to bend over and grab their ankles while a priest or a nun hit them repeatedly on the backside with a two-by-four. Sometimes the clergy forced the other children to beat up the troublemaker, and if anyone refused to participate, he would be next.

Gracie had already endured plenty of corporal punishment. She'd been slapped so many times she had lost count, she'd been made to scrub the floor on her hands and knees until she could hardly stand up, and she'd been locked in a closet for twenty-four hours without food, water or toilet facilities. For what? For being a child.

She sat alone in that classroom for what seemed an eternity until she heard footsteps approaching. She shut her eyes tight and reached in her pocket. Clutching her rosary, she said a silent prayer.

The door opened slowly, but Gracie refused to open her eyes.

"Mary Josephine?" It was Sister Margaret. Gracie exhaled with relief and looked up into the face of the only nun who had ever shown her any kindness.

"Come, child."

They walked down the long hall toward the Mother Superior's office, and Gracie was certain she would be slapped and lectured and made to do the worst possible chores in the whole orphanage. But Sister Margaret stopped and rested her hand on Gracie's shoulder. "Let's walk outside for a moment."

The sister knew a shortcut, an escape route that not even Gracie had found – a passage which brought them through another hallway to the back of the building and out to a meager vegetable garden. Gracie looked up with a question in her eyes, but the nun put her finger to her lips.

"Just listen," she whispered. "Wherever you go, whatever family takes you next, you must try always to do your best, and to behave as our Holy Mother would wish. Things will not always be as they are now. Do you understand?"

Gracie nodded. Sister Margaret looked at her for a long moment and then gently led her back to the Mother Superior's office.

"Come in," barked Mother Eugenia when she saw them standing in her doorway. "You!" She pointed at Gracie. "Stand right here." Gracie stepped in front of the Mother Superior's desk and stared at the wall.

"Sister Margaret," continued the Mother Superior, "You will leave for Buffalo tomorrow. The Immaculate Heart of Mary Orphans Home is ready to receive you. We feel it will be a more suitable environment for you, as your good nature prevents you from carrying out the discipline St. Joseph's requires."

Sister Margaret nodded and bowed her head. The Mother Superior cleared her throat. "Thank you, sister, for your service here."

Sister Margaret left the room without a word.

"As for you…" The Mother Superior picked up her ruler and slapped it on her palm. "I find it hard to understand how you could not manage to behave yourself for even *one week* with the Cotter family. You will *not* disappoint us again."

CHAPTER TWENTY-TWO

It was not Grace's intention to disappoint anyone. She was just trying to get by. The stories she heard from other foster children who were returned to the orphanage were often more frightening than what went on inside the walls of St. Joseph's. Some were physically abused, some sexually abused, and nearly all were used for physical labor unfit for children.

There was no government protection, and no child labor laws to speak of. Children's labor was necessary for commerce. In fact, the president of Merchants Woolen Company declared, "There is a certain class of labor in mills where there is not as much muscular exercise required as a child would put forth in play, and a child can do it about as well as a grown person... There is such thing as too much education for working people sometimes. I have seen cases where young people are spoiled for labor by... too much refinement."

Such was the prevailing sentiment of the day. Certainly, there was no department of children's services. Orphans were at the mercy of the foster family. What went on in a private home was nobody's business.

The Vernors had agreed to take Gracie as their newest foster child. They lived in a one-story clapboard house on the outskirts of

Wattsburg, near the Allegheny River. It took the better part of the day to get there by horse and buggy, and by nightfall Gracie had had plenty of time to compose herself. She would follow Sister Margaret's advice. She would allow herself no angry outbursts. She would not speak unless spoken to, and if anyone made a comment about her parents, she would pretend she hadn't heard.

Since the mid-1800s, when Wattsburg had been a thriving nexus of stagecoach traffic, the Vernor family had owned and operated the general mercantile. When Gracie came to live with them, the town was no longer in its heyday, but the third generation of Vernors had hung onto the store and managed to sell a great variety of items, from hammers and nails to flour and sorghum. Mrs. Vernor was a doughy woman whose eyes were set in a permanent squint. Her husband was a small man who chewed and spit tobacco. The secret of the Vernors' success was child labor. They had no children of their own, so they acquired foster children and put them to work.

The interior of the store was lit with kerosene lamps. Grace could hear the clink of metal on metal as Mrs. Vernor brought her inside. "That's Phil, and that's Molly," she said, pointing to a boy and girl who were picking nails out of a box and dropping them in tin cans according to size. The young workers looked up and nodded and went back to sorting nails. Gracie was hungry and wondered if she would get to eat any supper. She would not. Mrs. Vernor showed her a pallet with a straw mattress at the back of the store. "You'll sleep there," was all she said.

From dawn until dusk, the three foster children were kept busy. They attended the local elementary school for a few hours each day, much to Mr. and Mrs. Vernors' distress. The town of Wattsburg had a bluestocking busybody who made sure all school-age children took their places in the schoolhouse. The rest of the time, Gracie, Phil and Molly swept floors, whitewashed walls and fences, plucked chickens, packed and unpacked boxes, climbed ladders and stocked shelves. In addition to all these chores, Mrs. Vernor put Gracie in charge of cleaning up Mr. Vernor's gobs of tobacco juice.

Gracie's few hours at school were the best part of her day. She was a good student; she enjoyed reading and learned quickly. But all too soon, the bell rang and she had to return to the myriad menial tasks at Vernors' General Mercantile. She maintained her vow of silence. This wasn't difficult; Phil and Molly seemed to have taken a similar vow. They were brother and sister and shared the same wooden demeanor and empty stare. When Mr. and Mrs. Vernor issued the daily orders, the siblings nodded and set to work. Gracie followed their lead.

Until the day she had to climb the tall ladder and put cans of condensed milk on the top shelf. Normally, Phil was the one who climbed the ladder to stock the upper shelves. He was a strong, nimble boy, able to sling a box of canned milk over one shoulder and shinny up the ladder, one-handed. But Phil was in the backyard slaughtering chickens when the shipment arrived. Gracie was down on her hands and knees on the front porch, scrubbing brown goo off the floorboards and feeling a little sick to her stomach.

"Mary Josephine!" Mrs. Vernor screeched. "Get these cans on those shelves. Now!"

"Yes, ma'am," said Gracie, glad for a break from this disgusting task.

She tried to shoulder the box of cans as she'd seen Phil do, but lost her balance when she stepped on the first rung of the ladder. The box fell open and cans of condensed milk went rolling across the floor.

"Clumsy girl!" cried Mrs. Vernor. "Why don't you just take them up, one at a time?!"

Gracie pursed her lips, fighting the torrent of words that welled up inside her. She picked up a can and climbed to the top of the ladder, placing the can on the shelf. She climbed back down and picked up another can. She stuffed two more cans in the front of her dress and climbed back up. As she placed the cans on the shelf, she started to feel dizzy. She looked down and saw Mrs. Vernor squinting up at her with a peculiar smile on her face.

Suddenly she was overcome by a wave of nausea. The floor looked so far away.

Mrs. Vernor was clapping her hands. "Come, come, we haven't got all day!"

Gracie gripped the ladder with both hands and willed her legs to descend, rung by rung by rung. When she got to the bottom, she felt the contents of her stomach rise and tried to make a beeline for the door. But Mrs. Vernor grabbed her by the arm and Gracie threw up, making a direct hit on the woman's right shoe.

Shortly thereafter, she was sent back to St. Joseph's.

CHAPTER TWENTY-THREE

It was 1909 and Grace had just turned sixteen. The O'Malleys had not taken her in to share warmth and comfort of a convivial home; this foster family needed a maid and couldn't afford to pay a regular maid's wages. They weren't terrible people, but they weren't especially kind to her either.

"Mary Josephine! This floor needs to be scrubbed again!"

Grace followed Mrs. O'Malley's voice to the kitchen where she saw a perfectly clean floor, a floor she had scrubbed that very morning.

"Yes, ma'am," she said dully. Grace went to the service porch for the bucket and mop.

"You know, Mary Josephine," said Mrs. O'Malley, "we are all sick and tired of your sullen attitude."

"Yes, ma'am," said Grace as she added a splash of lye to the water.

"In fact, Mr. O'Malley says we should send you back to the orphanage and get us a cheerful girl."

Grace said nothing. She had already made her decision. After Mrs. O'Malley left the kitchen she whispered it to herself. *I am leaving tonight.*

This was Grace's fifteenth foster home and she had had enough.

Erie, Pennsylvania, was a bustling town – a railroad hub and center of trade on Lake Erie, with a population over fifty thousand people – but it was too small a town for Grace. That night she packed her few belongings and waited until the O'Malleys had gone to bed. The back door creaked as she stepped out onto the porch. She paused, holding her breath, to make certain no one had heard the sound. Then she made her way on foot to the railroad station and climbed into a boxcar on a southbound train to Pittsburgh.

The boxcar was empty but had recently been full of livestock. It stank. But it was still far better than going back to St. Joseph's. The first time she had set eyes on that place, it had terrified her. She was only four years old and it was the biggest building she'd ever seen: dark and medieval-looking with a huge cross that cast eerie shadows on the ground. Life inside that building had terrified her almost every day she spent inside its walls.

Grace settled herself on a pile of hay in the corner of the boxcar and shut her eyes against the vision of that unholy place. For close to eleven years – most of her childhood – she had been shuffled back and forth between various foster homes and the asylum. She never lasted very long with any of the foster families. Each time she was returned to St. Joseph's, the nuns blamed her for not trying hard enough to be agreeable, and they treated her even more harshly. As she grew older, the punishments grew more drastic. It was almost as if the nuns knew she had grown a thicker skin and disciplined her all the harder.

No matter what happened next in her young life, she knew she would *never* go back to that place. She would put it all behind her now, and lock all those memories in a secret vault. She had neither money nor strategy. Her only plan was to escape... for once and for all.

Just before dawn, the boxcar carrying Grace arrived in Pittsburgh. The railway terminal looked enormous, dark and grimy. She stood on tiptoe and looked for trees — trees meant shelter, neighborhoods and people. Before the sun was far above the horizon, Grace had walked to the center of town where tree-lined streets of stately brownstones stretched out in every direction. She looked down at her flimsy woolen dress and her scuffed shoes, bits of hay still stuck to their soles, and darted around a corner into an empty alley. She ran her hand along the high brick wall and paused to plan her next move.

Suddenly the morning quiet gave way to the pounding of hoofs; Grace turned around to see a horse-drawn cart clattering towards her up the alley. Looking for a quick escape route, she saw that the tall wooden gate in the brick wall stood partway open and she pushed her way through.

On the other side of this brick wall stood the Browning house. Grace stared in awe at the green lawn and flowerbeds and imposing two-story house and leaned against the brickwork to catch her breath. She ran her fingers through her hair and brushed the hay from her shoes. She realized she had had nothing to eat or drink since she'd left Erie. When she saw the back door open and a young girl in a maid's uniform come outside with a bin full of trash, she straightened up, brushed the dust from her skirt and stepped forward. *Perhaps she will give me a sip of water.*

"There you are!" said the young maid. "Come this way, please."

Grace uncertainly followed the girl to the back door. "Wait here, please," said the maid, closing the door on her.

Strange, thought Grace. But she did as she was told and waited. Suddenly the door swung open, and another woman in a maid's uniform, an older woman with grey hair twisted up on top of her head, stood there peering at her.

"I'm sorry to bother you --" Grace began.

"Please come in," said the woman. "The lady of the house will be with you shortly."

Grace was stunned, but she followed the woman into the kitchen.

"Mrs. Browning and her daughter have been through a difficult time: her husband recently passed away." She turned around and looked closely into Grace's face. "We all tread lightly around the Missus."

"Yes, ma'am," said Grace doubtfully.

"You can call me Jane."

Mrs. Browning was sitting alone in her formal dining room, fretting and worrying. Since her husband had died, her daughter Margaret refused to leave her bedroom or even speak to her. Even worse, her household had gone to pieces. Millicent Browning's response to her husband's death was to seize control and rule with an iron fist. She had been a rather bossy woman to begin with, but the loss of her husband had turned her into an insufferable dictator. Several of the servants had quit, unable to cope with the widow's autocratic management style. After a month of interviewing domestics, she was desperate: her bed had gone unmade for two whole days, and an inefficient household was her worst nightmare. But she refused to fail in her own home.

"And who have we here?" Millicent Browning asked in an imperious tone.

"The new girl from the agency, Mrs. Browning," said Jane, nodding curtly and exiting the room.

Grace eyed the well-dressed matron with perfect posture sitting at the head of the table, a silver teapot and half-empty breakfast dishes spread before her, and stood mute, her hands clasped in front of her.

"What is your name, young lady?" said Mrs. Browning, loudly and distinctly. She wondered if perhaps this girl was backward or hard of hearing.

"Mary Dodson," answered Grace in a clear voice, surprised and rather pleased with herself that she didn't have to give her full baptismal name. Mary Dodson would do just fine.

"Can you clean and keep a house?" she asked.

Grace nodded. "Yes, ma'am." Mrs. Browning's pigeon-like chest expanded as she took a deep breath and then exhaled with relief. "Excellent!"

So Mary Dodson was hired and moved into the servant's quarters that very morning. For the first time in her life, she had her very own room — a real room, with four walls and a door! It was small, but it was all hers. Her first assignment was upstairs chambermaid and she would actually be *paid* for her labor.

Things were looking up. Grace was thankful but she did not rejoice. A life filled almost entirely with loss and hardship had taught her that usually things get bad and then they get worse. She would be cautious and take each day as it came. But there would be no going back.

CHAPTER TWENTY-FOUR

As upstairs chambermaid, Grace was responsible for making up the bedchambers, all eight of them. Although only two of the bedchambers were being used – Mrs. Browning's and her daughter's – Millicent Browning decreed that all the bedding had to be changed weekly, regardless of whether anybody slept in it or not. That was simply proper housekeeping. Her staff thought she was crazy but it kept them busy and employed.

Gracie had no qualms about the task. If there was one thing she knew how to do and do well, it was how to make a bed, with squared corners and sheets pulled so tight you could bounce a coin off of them. But before sending her new employee upstairs, Millicent Browning delivered her standard speech on proper protocol for all servants working in her home:

"Domestics do not engage in conversation with members of the family. Do not talk to any guest in the house, unless the guest addresses you first. In fact, I don't even want to see the help engage in conversation with each other. Is that understood?"

Grace nodded her head; she understood. This would not be a problem, since Grace had long since given up making conversation; the social impulse had been effectively beaten out of her at St. Joseph's.

"All bedchambers that are in use – that would be my own and that of my daughter Margaret – must be refreshed and made up daily during breakfast hour. Without fail. I may want to return to my room after the morning meal. If I find my bed has not been properly made up, well..." Mrs. Browning paused dramatically. "There will be severe consequences."

Grace understood the nature of severe consequences and would do everything in her power to avoid them in her new job.

This was certainly the finest, grandest house Grace had ever seen. The floors were polished oak, the ceilings were high and many of the windowpanes were leaded glass. And the furniture! Every piece upholstered in such soft, shiny silk brocade that Grace didn't even want to touch it, let alone even think about sitting on it. Not that she'd ever dare.

That morning, her first morning at her new job, Grace had made up Mrs. Browning's room and freshened the other rooms upstairs. She walked briskly down the hall to make up the last bedroom. She felt strong and efficient, even though her new uniform fit her like a gunny sack, sagging on her thin frame. Enjoying a growing sense of confidence in her new job, she bolted through the last door and headed straight for the pile of sheets and blankets in the middle of the unmade bed.

When she yanked the bedding to the floor, she was startled to see a girl lying underneath the pile. The girl on the bed was even more startled. She sat straight up and glared at the intruder.

Grace screamed and almost jumped out of her shoes.

Oh, Lord, now I'm done for... Frozen in fear, Grace opened her mouth but was unable to utter a sound. She waited for the pretty auburn-haired girl on the bed to leap up and pounce on her. But the girl on the bed didn't move a muscle… she just sat there staring at Grace, and Grace stared back.

Meg Browning had not left her room, or her bed, since her father had passed away, except on a couple of rare occasions when her mother was able to coax her out. She had cocooned herself in her bedclothes and a deep depression, and her mother's well-intentioned intrusions were no comfort at all. She just wanted to be left alone.

She studied the terrified look on the pretty young blonde standing before her. Then she noticed the girl's uniform was two sizes too big and started to laugh. It began as a giggle that, try as she might, she couldn't stifle. Soon she was overcome by uncontrollable laughter.

Perhaps it was nothing more than the release of weeks of tension and sorrow that had built up inside; whatever it was, it was finally out and it felt good. Meg Browning fell back on the bed and rolled with laughter. She laughed so hard she clutched her sides. The wonderful thing about laughter is that it's infectious: Grace forgot how frightened she'd been and now she started to laugh for the first time in years. In fact, she couldn't remember ever having laughed like this. Clutching the bedclothes, she fell to her knees, dissolved in sidesplitting giggles.

Finally Meg got out of bed, looking down at the girl in the ill-fitting maid's uniform who was doubled over on the floor.

"Who are you? And how *old* are you?"

Grace struggled to her feet. "I'm the new chambermaid. My name's Mary... well, my real name's Grace, and I'm eighteen."

"You are *not!* You look like you're twelve." The oversized uniform made this new chambermaid look like she was playing dress-up in her mother's clothes. "How old are you, *really?*"

"How old are *you?*" Grace replied, a bit defensively.

"Seventeen," said Meg.

Grace glanced up quickly into Meg's eyes – large emerald green pools that faded into brown – and then looked down at the floor. "Sixteen," she said softly. "Please don't tell on me. I gotta keep this job. I told the Missus I was eighteen."

Nothing good ever lasts, thought Grace. She was already imagining herself back on the streets of Pittsburgh in her old clothes.

"And she believed you?" Meg asked, plunking herself back down on the bed.

Grace nodded and kept her eyes cast downward.

Suddenly Meg felt something almost like pity for this girl, a girl almost her age who had blundered unknowingly into her solitude and made her laugh for the first time in a very long time. "Why the two names?" she asked gently.

Grace stole a quick glance into Meg's face. The combination of her warm green eyes and the genuine caring in her voice posed no threat.

"I'm an orphan," Grace said. "The nuns changed my name to Mary Josephine." She made a sour face and Meg gave her a sympathetic smile.

"That's not as bad as my name," replied Meg. "Mahhh-garet

Winifred! That's how my mother pronounces it."

Grace smiled. "My real name's Grace, but nobody knows that. I like Grace better."

She looked up shyly and saw the twinkle in Meg's eyes. "I like Grace better, too," said Meg, extending her hand. "My name is Meg, not Mah-garet." The girls shook hands and sealed their formal introduction. "I guess I have two names as well."

Grace nodded and smiled. "I like Meg better, too."

"You know, Grace, I've never met an orphan before. What happened to your parents?"

The smile left Grace's face like the sun going into eclipse and she looked down at her feet. Instantly, Meg knew she'd been rude to ask and felt bad for the girl. She quickly changed the subject back to names.

"I decided to call myself Meg because of my mother. She can be so pretentious… the way she calls me Mah-garet is so irritating."

Meg's attempt to lighten the moment wasn't working. She felt Grace slipping away but didn't know how to re-engage her. "You know as household staff, you're not supposed to converse with me. You do know that, don't you, Grace?"

"Then don't scare the livin' daylights outta me again," snapped Grace. She was in no mood to be scolded for something that had not been her fault.

Meg started to giggle again. "I won't, I promise!" She stood up and took a step toward Grace who was still looking upset.

"You must believe me, Grace. Please?" said Meg and she reached out her hands. Then Grace smiled and said, "I believe you…

Mah-garet!" The two girls dissolved into giggles again. It did feel good to laugh.

"But seriously, Grace," Meg continued. "If you want to keep your job – and I really hope you do – you must never speak to me when my mother is around."

Grace nodded, and in that moment, the two girls made a silent, solemn pact and began an extraordinary friendship that they kept entirely secret from the rest of the household

"Good afternoon, Mother," said Meg as she entered the dining room for lunch. Millicent Browning almost dropped her spoon, so surprised was she to see her daughter, not only up and dressed but joining her for the midday meal.

"G-g-good afternoon, Margaret," Mrs. Browning stammered. "I'm surprised... no, I am delighted to see you, dear!" A thousand questions popped into the lady's head but she thought better of asking anything that might cause her daughter to plunge back into the depression that had gripped her for months. "Thank heaven for small mercies," she said to herself; she was simply glad to see her daughter downstairs and dressed in something other than a nightgown.

Mrs. Browning directed Jane, the senior housekeeper who had been with the Brownings the longest, to bring her daughter's lunch. "And do be quick about it!" Millicent Browning barely touched her own food; she just sat at the table and beamed at her daughter.

The same scene was repeated, more or less, at dinnertime, only Jane had asked the new girl to help with the serving dishes. Grace, known to her new employer and co-workers as Mary, quietly placed dishes, cups, saucers and serving platters in front of Mrs. Browning and her newfound friend, all the while keeping her eyes averted from Meg's. She felt invisible. Mrs. Browning conversed with her daughter as if the servants were not even there. Actually, Mrs. Browning did most of the talking – everything she had been saving up to say to her daughter during the months that Meg had refused to leave her room came out in a torrent. She didn't know what it was that had brought her daughter out of that dark place – she was just glad to have her back.

When it was time for Grace to remove the dishes from the dining table, Mrs. Browning went to the kitchen to have a word with the cook. As soon as the lady's back was turned, Meg coughed loudly, catching Grace's eye. Meg tilted her head upward and pointed toward the ceiling, mouthing the words, "My room, nine o'clock."

Grace nodded and without a word carried the dishes to the kitchen where Mrs. Browning was handing the cook a shopping list. The lady of the house turned to see her new employee carefully set the dirty dishes on the sideboard. She smiled with self-satisfaction. *Thank goodness this house is back in order and the bedchambers are being made up properly.* It would never have occurred to her to tell the new girl personally how pleased she was.

CHAPTER TWENTY-FIVE

That night, Grace climbed the servants' stairs to Meg's room and knocked softly on the door. When the door opened, she was surprised to see how enormous Meg's room really was. She couldn't help thinking, *I grew up in a room not even half this big, and crammed with twenty other girls.*

"Come in, please sit down," said Meg, gesturing to the bed.

Now that Grace had gotten over her fright and nerves, she noticed the expensive furniture, the rich brocaded fabric of the floor-to-ceiling draperies, and the vast collection of china dolls – each one dressed in a miniature costume, a perfect representation of a different foreign land.

"You can close your mouth, Grace," said Meg. "Unless you were hoping to catch a fly or two."

Embarrassed, Grace clamped her jaws shut and Meg giggled. There was something about this new girl that Meg liked and she wanted to put her at her ease. She went to the shelf of china dolls and selected one.

"Here… do you like her? She was always my favorite," she said as she handed the doll to Grace. It was a Heidi doll, with a starched white pinafore and golden braids.

"She's awful pretty," said Grace, gingerly taking the doll and holding it at arm's length.

"Did they let you have dolls at the orphanage?" asked Meg.

"Oh, no," said Grace.

"What was it like, living in an orphanage?"

Grace quickly handed the doll back and lowered her eyes to the floor.

Meg caught the sudden shift in mood. "Here, let me show you something." She went to an ornate carved bureau, withdrew a soft, pale blue pile of wool from one of the drawers and handed it to Grace.

"Sometimes this house gets a little drafty, especially in the winter. You might want to wear this under your uniform. Or you can wear it under your nightgown. I do that sometimes." She held the blue chemise up to Grace's shoulders. "This will fit you perfectly."

"Oh, I couldn't," said Grace.

"Yes, you could," said Meg, her jaw set firmly, her eyes flashing with determination. "My mother would have an absolute fit if you caught cold. If she saw you sneezing on her breakfast dishes, why... You could lose your job."

Grace ran her hand over the soft woolen garment. "Well, since you put it that way." Then they both giggled, and the tension vanished.

"We really must do something about that uniform you're wearing," said Meg. "You're positively swimming in it."

Grace gave her a questioning look. "It's all right, just a bit big," she said.

"That's what I mean. I'll speak to Jane tomorrow and see if she has something smaller. In the meantime..."

Meg took some safety pins from a porcelain bowl on the bureau.

"Stand up!" she commanded.

Grace did as she was told and Meg deftly pinned the uniform in two sections at the back, creating darts that folded the fabric neatly at the waistline. Now the dress almost hugged the figure inside it.

"Pshaw!" said Grace as she turned to look at herself in the mirror.

"That's much better, isn't it?"

"Yes, ma'am," said Grace.

Meg balled her fists and placed them on her hips. "No, Grace! When we're here in my room, you must never call me 'ma'am.' I'm Meg. Remember? My name is Meg."

"I'll do that," said Grace, "So long as you remember to call me Mary downstairs. They all know me as Mary, ya know."

"I'll certainly do that. It will be fun, won't it? You and I, the only ones who know your real identity!" Meg clapped her hands at the intrigue of it all.

But Grace wasn't sure if "fun" was the right word for it.

During the day, Meg and Grace never spoke and seldom even glanced at one another. They followed Mrs. Browning's protocol to the letter. But every night, after the rest of the household had retired for the evening, Grace would sneak up the servants' stairs to Meg's room and for an hour or so, the girls would meet as equals. They talked about what had happened that day and exchanged household gossip, and Meg felt comfortable enough to use Grace as a sounding board when she needed to let off steam about her mother.

Grace was a sympathetic listener. In fact, she adored listening to Meg talk; she loved the way Meg strung words together, the way she could perform spot-on imitations of people and make them come to life right there in her bedroom – especially Mrs. Browning. The girls laughed and giggled like the best of friends and in time became as close, or maybe even closer than sisters.

There was only one topic of conversation that was off-limits: Grace's past. In the beginning, Meg tried to get her to speak about her parents and what life was like at the orphanage. Grace would simply shut down. Her eyes would grow distant, and then she'd drop her head and set her mouth in a firm line. She could not and would not allow herself to revisit those memories. The mask of self-protection descended so quickly, it was as if a switch had flicked and changed her personality. Finally, Meg let it drop. She much preferred the other Grace, the girl with whom she could share stories and laugh.

The miracle was that Grace could laugh at all. After seeing her beloved Poppa carted away to jail, her mother's abandonment, losing her sister Linnie to an adoptive family, and then being told her little brother Jimmy was dead, by the age of six Grace had stopped smiling altogether. There was nothing left to smile about, not the tiniest bit of joy left. The ensuing years were all about survival. She never believed that any sort of happiness could last and therefore never allowed herself to dream about the future. Instead, she developed an absolute genius for day-to-day survival, by building a solid wall around herself and maintaining a blank expression.

Little by little, Meg found the crack in the wall.

CHAPTER TWENTY-SIX

"I'd like to be just like you," Grace confessed to Meg during one of their late night sessions. "You're so... so..." She searched for the right words to describe her friend.

Meg jumped in to finish the sentence. "Beautiful, elegant and graceful?" She straightened her posture as she spoke, cocked her left shoulder forward, and tilted her chin ever so slightly.

"Yeah! Beautiful, elegant and graceful." The words sounded strange in Grace's mouth; she could not pronounce them with the same sense of confidence that Meg did. She was, in fact, in awe of the way Meg could always find the right words to say and deliver them with such ease.

"Well, if your mother slapped you on the back every time you slouched or said 'yeah,' you *would* be just like me," said Meg. "Sit up straight, stand up straight, don't put your elbows on the table, never say 'I'm full,' when you've had enough to eat... I am always annoyed at constantly being corrected!"

Grace looked down at the floor out of habit, as if *she* were being scolded.

"Grace?"

Grace looked up.

"First, don't say 'yeah' ever again. It's 'yes.' The word is *'yes.'* And why do you keep doing that?"

Grace looked confused. "Doing what?"

"You are always looking down at the floor. It's not going anywhere."

The habit of looking down had been with Grace since her early days at St. Joseph's. As a small child she thought that if she avoided eye contact she could make herself invisible. When she grew older, she realized she couldn't really disappear, but she could circumvent some nasty consequences if she didn't look someone in the eye – particularly if that someone was the Mother Superior.

Meg stepped closer and gently lifted Grace's chin. "Hold your head up high, Grace. Don't be afraid to look a person directly in the eye when you're engaged in conversation. Unless, of course, you're flirting with a gentleman. In that case, looking down at the floor is quite acceptable."

"Flirting?" Grace had never heard the word.

"We'll save that for another time," replied Meg with a smile. "Look up. Let them see your eyes. Besides, *your* eyes could melt ice."

Grace blushed.

"When you look directly into someone's eyes," Meg continued, "you're in control, and believe me, they'll listen. If you don't want to answer a particular question, you may look down; that will let them think you're either embarrassed or the answer is just too painful to give."

Grace's head was spinning with all this advice, but she listened and memorized every word.

"And one more thing," said Meg. *"Stand up straight!* Your mother should have slapped you on the back for slouching."

"I don't have a mother," said Grace, squaring her shoulders and standing erect.

"I'm sorry," said Meg, chagrined that she'd made another thoughtless remark. "But didn't the nuns at the orphanage slap you on the back for slouching?"

"They slapped me for lots of things, but never just 'cause I slouched."

Meg didn't know how to respond to this; she didn't want to pry, knowing every time she tried to open the door to the past, Grace would slam it shut in her face. She decided to try another tactic. "Then let me help you. I'll pretend to be your mother."

Grace winced, but didn't say anything. She was curious to know exactly how Meg thought she could help.

"I'll pretend to be your mother, at least at night. That means I'll slap you when you slouch. And correct your grammar. And in no time at all, you'll be just like me — stiff, straight and sore, but speaking perfect English."

Grace was stunned. She had never met anyone who took an interest in her. Here was this lovely girl who lived a fairytale life, who had beautiful clothes and plenty of money, who went to school because she wanted to, not because she *had* to — and she actually cared whether Grace said "yes," instead of "yeah," and "isn't" instead of "inn't." Every evening the lessons continued: Meg corrected Grace's grammar and diction and pronunciation. Grace was a quick study and eagerly absorbed her new vocabulary the way a drowning man gasps for air.

Her posture, however, was a tougher nut to crack.

"Stand up straight, you're slouching!" said Meg.

Grace was startled into an upright position and groaned. Why, oh, why was this so difficult to remember?

"A lady never slouches," added Meg, imitating her mother's pretentious cadence. "Oh, I wish I could be with you all day long, Grace. That's when you need to be reminded."

"You're right," said Grace. "I guess I just go back to my own ways when you're not around."

Suddenly Meg's eyes lit up. "Wait! I have an idea." Using an old, soft leather belt, she strapped a yardstick to Grace's back. "This is what you'll do, Grace. You'll wear this under your uniform. You'll have no choice but to stand straight."

Meg was proud of her brilliant plan but she wasn't there to hear the loud snap the next morning when Grace bent over to dust a footstool.

"Mercy sakes, what was that?" called Jane from another room.

"Nothing," called Grace, shaking the broken yardstick out of the back of her uniform. By the time Jane and the other downstairs maid Lucille came pounding into the parlor, Grace had stashed her makeshift posture-aid in the fireplace.

"I could have sworn I heard something break in here," said Jane, eyeing Grace with suspicion.

"Nothing's broke… er, I mean broken," said Grace, turning her attention to the mantelpiece. She ran her dustcloth back and forth over the mantelpiece, until Jane and Lucille finally left the room.

CHAPTER TWENTY-SEVEN

Meg brought home a sufficient number of yardsticks from school to cure her protégée of slouching. Every evening Grace got a new yardstick. That first week she broke every single one. Housework requires bending from the waist and the mysterious snaps and cracks alarmed the other servants. They could never discover the source of the sound, but it always seemed to happen in Grace's vicinity. Grace was always found to be working hard, a neutral expression on her face. She'd look up blandly when someone asked about the noise and say, "No, I didn't hear anything."

The yardsticks worked their magic and before too long Grace was naturally standing straighter and walking taller. In fact, her walk had become stately. Meg was thrilled.

"Look at you! Walk across the room for me." Meg clapped her hands and Grace walked gracefully from one end of Meg's bedroom to the other.

"It really makes such a difference, Grace. Do you feel different?"

Grace shrugged her shoulders. "Maybe. I know my back feels better without a yardstick sticking into it!"

She noticed the bed and floor were strewn with Meg's beautiful clothes and cardboard boxes. "What are you doing? Where are you going?" She felt an old, familiar panic rise inside her but tried to keep her voice even and calm.

"I'm not going anywhere," replied Meg as she picked up a skirt, folded it and placed it in one of the boxes. "Mother and I had our final fittings today for our new fall wardrobes. They'll be arriving in a few days from Boston, so I have to clean out all my old clothes to make room for the new ones. One does have to be fashionable, you know."

The panic subsided and the color returned to Grace's face. "No, I don't know," she said, looking around the room at the abundance of clothes. "But they're all still perfect, like new... and so beautiful."

She couldn't grasp the notion that anyone could discard perfectly good clothing. The bed was piled with evening gowns, day dresses, skirts, blouses, hats and shoes, and none of them looked as if they had been worn more than a few times. She sat down on the edge of the bed and picked up a silk blouse. The hand-stitched label sewn inside read: *Beacon Place Couture • Boston.*

"I thought your clothes were from Paris."

"Well, almost," said Meg. "The designs are from Paris, but they're actually made in Boston. There's a clothier there, a husband and wife team, a lovely couple. They import originals direct from Paris – Worth and Poiret – and recreate exact copies of them. So mine, I'm afraid, are really only copies, but they are very good copies."

This was astounding new information, and Grace filed it away. She had never heard of Worth or Poiret, but she liked the way the names sounded. She also liked the notion that people could take somebody else's idea and make it their own, like this couple in Boston. Imagine having the skill to do that!

"Go on," Grace said.

"The wife is one of the best seamstresses in the world. At least that's what I've been told. Her work is exquisite. Here, look!" Meg held up a peach-colored silk gown with dozens and dozens of tiny covered buttons sewn from the neckline to the hem.

Grace took the gown and held it toward the light, then examined each of the little buttons.

"The workmanship is so good that no one would even suspect they're not Paris originals. Besides," Meg said, taking the gown from Grace and carefully folding it into a box, "we couldn't afford the originals. You'd have to be a Vanderbilt."

Grace didn't know what a Vanderbilt was, but she made a mental note to find out.

"Don't tell my mother I told you; she likes everyone to believe they are originals."

"Don't you remember?" asked Grace. "I'm not supposed to speak to your mother."

Meg laughed. "Oh, of course, I forgot! But honestly, my mother insists that we cut out the labels before they're donated to keep it our secret." Grace saw the pile of labels Meg had already removed from many of the garments. She picked up another gown and tentatively brushed the fabric against her cheek.

Watching Grace, seeing her face transform at the soft touch of the silken fabric, reminded Meg how meaningless and self-indulgent it must seem to replace one's entire wardrobe every new season. "The clothes don't go to waste," she said, trying to redeem herself, to explain away a tradition that had always made sense to her. "We donate them to charity, to help the poor. Of course I don't know where the poor would wear some of these."

She picked up an exquisite orange and crimson gown of organza silk with glass beading and held it against her body. "A little dressy for a trip to the fish market, perhaps?"

Oh, dear, why did I say that? She really must think I'm the most frivolous person who ever lived, thought Meg.

Grace just stared at her. What Grace was really thinking was: *I have one dress, one skirt and one blouse, and I've never thought of myself as poor.*

"It's beautiful," was all she could say.

The last thing in the world Meg wanted to do was embarrass her friend. But at this moment, in her room full of surfeit, it was Meg who was embarrassed. She held the gown out to Grace. "Here, try it on."

"No, I couldn't." Grace shook her head and refused to take the gown from Meg's hands.

"Yes, you could."

Grace crossed her arms in front of her chest and looked at the floor. Meg burst out laughing. "Now, really, Grace.... What harm is there in a little game of dress-up?"

She picked up another gown from the pile on the bed, a slate blue silk, and slipped it on. "I always loved this one," she remarked as she spun around the room. "See how the hem flares?" She twirled again, humming *The Blue Danube* as if she were at a dance.

Grace was mesmerized. Meg seized the moment and, still

humming the waltz, unfastened the girl's uniform. The shapeless thing dropped in a heap around Grace's feet. Meg took Grace's hand, as if bidding her to join the dance, and Grace stepped out of the pile of grey fabric. Then, in one swift motion, Meg lowered the orange and crimson gown over Grace's head and fastened the buttons.

"There!" she cried. "Come, look at yourself!"

She led her friend over to the mirror. "It fits you perfectly, my dear. Who would have thought we were the same size?"

Grace couldn't believe her eyes. *Who is that elegant lady in the mirror?*

That evening, the boxes of clothes marked "For Charity" somehow found their way down to Grace's little room in the servants' quarters.

CHAPTER TWENTY-EIGHT

Grace didn't think she'd ever be able to fall asleep that night. She lay in bed replaying the entire evening in her mind: Meg leading her around the room, first a waltz, then a box step. With every costume change, she'd change the tune – now humming Schubert's *Valses Sentimentales*, now humming Chopin's *Minute Waltz* – and every few minutes, she would coax Grace into slipping into another silk confection.

"Try *this* one on," said Meg, helping Grace out of the orange gown and into a royal blue sweep of chiffon and feathers. Grace couldn't imagine where one would possibly wear something so fine, but Meg's enthusiasm for playing dress-up and twirling around her bedroom was infectious. "If anything," Grace thought to herself, "I *am* learning how to dance!"

After the girls had tried on all the ball gowns, Meg made Grace try on skirts and jackets, blouses and afternoon tea dresses, as she chattered away about the different fabrics and styles. Grace began to learn the language of fashion: taffeta, voile, serge, piqué, foulard, broadcloth and chambray. She repeated each word, committing it to memory.

It was uncanny how Meg's clothes fit her like a glove.

"Why don't *you* take these clothes? I can't believe how perfectly they fit you," said Meg. "I go for fitting after fitting to get them just right and you... you just step right into them."

Meg had only seen Grace in her nightgown and wearing her maid's uniform, a garment that wasn't designed to flatter any member of the Browning household staff's figure. She was astounded at how similarly they were built – they were the same height and had the same bone structure and slender waist.

"And what would I do with them?" asked Grace. "I don't go anywhere to wear clothes like these."

"Maybe not now," said Meg, picking up a wide-brimmed hat threaded with multicolored satin ribbons. "But you never know what the future holds." She put the hat on Grace's head and then held up a full-length day dress made of grey wool serge and detailed with the same multicolored ribbons sewn around the shoulders and hips. "See? They go together."

With the hat on her head, Grace stepped into the day dress.

"Now, let's fix your hair properly," said Meg. She removed the hat and pinned Grace's thick blond hair into a high chignon, then repositioned the hat at a smart angle.

Grace had taken one look at herself in the mirror and, from that moment on, had fallen in love with the idea of wearing hats.

Now, too excited to sleep, she propped herself up on one elbow and looked at the stack of boxes in the corner of the room. Not daring to turn on the light, not daring to draw attention to this most unusual thing that had happened – that *was happening* – Grace drew back the curtains and let in the moonlight. She opened one of the boxes and took out a hat, a wine-colored wool felt angular style with a single feather that swooped across the top.

Never in my life have I ever owned a hat… and now I have one for every day of the week!

Grace smiled to herself. Then she recalled the business of the shoes. When Meg had presented Grace with a pair of three-strap patent leather slippers, Grace had kicked off her serviceable brown lace-ups and two little balls of rolled-up newspaper had bounced out of her shoes and onto the carpet.

"What are these?"

"Oh!" cried Grace. She plucked the wads of newspaper from the floor and stuffed them back into her shoes.

"Do your shoes hurt you? You must tell me, Grace."

"No, no, it's not that. You see, well, look at my legs." Grace raised the hem of the jumper skirt she had just tried on.

"What about your legs?" asked Meg.

"They're bowed."

"I hadn't noticed. They look perfectly fine to me."

"Well, I've made them look better by stuffing paper in my shoes… like this." She showed Meg how she placed the homemade cushions inside each shoe, positioning them around the outside of each heel. "It keeps my ankles from turning out. If my ankles don't turn out, then the rest of my leg is straighter."

"That's ingenious!" cried Meg, clapping her hands. "But I can't have you stuffing newspaper into my patent leather slippers."

She promised Grace she would take all her cast-off shoes to the shoemaker and ask him to insert special pads in the inner sole.

Grace put the hat back in its box and then carefully, soundlessly stacked all the boxes in her tiny closet. She got back under the covers but left the curtains open, the better perhaps to see her thoughts. It had been months since Meg had slapped her on the back for slouching, or corrected her for dropping the "g" when she spoke of reading, sewing or singing. Meg had chastised her gently but firmly, repeating the proper pronunciations and then asking Grace to imitate her diction exactly.

Grace had never met anyone so kind and so generous. The last really kind and generous person she had known was her Poppa. But she had long ago stopped remembering him.

An eager student, Grace absorbed every piece of information Meg shared like a sponge, and like a mirror she copied Meg's every move and gesture. She'd even started to read the newspapers, slyly whisking them away when Mrs. Browning had finished reading the headlines and the society columns after breakfast. She had finally learned who the Vanderbilts were; at least one member of that illustrious and wealthy family was written about every week. Meg was only too pleased to enlighten her about other pillars of society – Astors and Belmonts and Whitneys, where they lived and *how* they lived, and, more importantly, how society worked. All the subtle dos and don'ts a young lady needed to know to navigate the waters of the upper crust.

Grace realized she had been holding her breath, thinking of all these things. She exhaled into the moonlit room and pulled the covers up to her chin. *Things are finally all right*, she thought. *As long as I don't do something foolish and lose my jo*b.

CHAPTER TWENTY-NINE

Meg and Grace thought they were hiding their friendship from everyone else in the house, but they both had a sneaking suspicion that Jane, the senior housekeeper, knew something was going on between the two. Jane had worked in service since she was a young girl. Like Grace, she had started as a chambermaid and over the years had held many jobs in many households. Although she was over sixty years of age, she walked with a spritely step and had the strength of a woman half her age. She wore her long grey hair in a thick braid across the crown of her head. This added several inches to her already considerable height and she used her stature to keep the younger, less experienced and less disciplined servants in line. She even held sway over the Brownings' butler who had served the family almost as long as she had.

Mrs. Browning owed the tidiness of her household to Jane, although she neither admitted nor acknowledged this. Jane didn't expect her to; she did her job for the wage, not for thanks or glory. Still, the tall woman with the lined face took great pride in following the established order of things; more than once she had taken one of the younger maids outside for a firm talking-to, and then shadowed her for the rest of the day to make sure the infraction was not repeated. Jane was nothing if not observant.

She had, in fact, noticed the changes in Mary Dodson just a few weeks after the girl had begun working for the Brownings. Jane could have sworn that Mary was standing up straighter and walking with an air of self-assurance, very unlike the average young chambermaid. She had also noticed the changes in Mary's speech: the Pennsylvania backwoods inflections were gone. The girl was actually speaking with the same precise diction as Meg Browning.

Even more, Jane had noticed an extraordinary change in Meg since the arrival of the new maid. Jane had been with the Browning family since Meg was a little girl, and she'd always felt responsible for her well-being, even though she knew it was not her place. The devastation and depression caused by Mr. Browning's death had hurt Jane almost as much as it hurt Meg, because Jane saw the bright, happy, carefree girl she'd always known disappear under a dark cloud. True, Meg was a spoiled only child who had always been given everything she had ever wanted; her doting father had seen to that. She was also a strong-willed girl – once she made up her mind, neither hell nor angels could change it.

But since Mary Dodson had joined the household, Jane had detected a softer side to Meg. She didn't know that Meg had changed her charity habits, but she had a suspicion: the stacks of boxes that used to leave Meg's room with the advent of each new fashion season had mysteriously stopped. Jane could only conclude that the girls had somehow made friends and that was perfectly all right with her... so long as Mrs. Browning didn't find out. Rules were rules, and Mrs. Browning's dictates were cast-iron: no fraternizing with staff!

One evening, Jane spied Meg tripping down the servants' stairs with a box in her arms.

"Oh! Good evening, Jane," said Meg.

Jane returned Meg's greeting with a curt nod. "Mary's room is the third door on the left," she said as she turned to go back upstairs.

Meg leaned against the wall to catch her breath and ponder how Jane had known what room she was looking for. The servants' hallway was stark with only one light fixture, and the walls were completely bare. Meg noticed there was not even any wallpaper in this part of the house. It had all seemed so much bigger and brighter when she was a little girl and would go running all over that big house, exploring the places her mother had forbidden her to go.

She pushed open the door to Grace's little room and shoved the box across the floor.

Later that night, Grace made her usual pilgrimage to her friend's room. "Thank you for the shoes, Meg. They fit just perfectly."

"The sacrifices I make for you, child," said Meg, dramatically throwing one arm across her brow in imitation of a melodramatic stage actress. "Jane saw me on the stairs."

"Oh, dear," said Grace. "Did she say anything?"

"Not a word."

"Do you think she would tell your mother?" Grace could see her whole life collapsing before her eyes.

"Don't be concerned, Grace. I highly doubt Jane would say anything, particularly since it is none of her business."

But Grace was concerned. Whether she imagined it or not, she had the distinct impression that Jane was watching her. She took extra care with all her household duties and made sure she responded to any of Jane's requests with a pleasant smile and an acquiescent nod. Since Jane's own room was several doors down the hall from hers, Grace's late night sorties up to Meg's room had not been difficult to manage. The girls kept to a routine: they would wait until Mrs. Browning had retired to her own bedroom – usually by nine-thirty, and then Grace would wait until she'd heard the other maids close their bedroom doors. The butler's quarters were on the other side of the house, next to the garage, so there was seldom any danger of running into him.

It was one of those clear, balmy summer nights when Grace opened her bedroom window to inhale the fragrant air. She could hear the house settling down, doors closing, other windows being cranked open to catch the fresh night breeze. Next door she heard Lucille, the downstairs maid, yawn loudly and then land with a thud on her squeaky mattress. Grace put on her robe and stepped into the hallway. All was still.

As she tiptoed toward the stairs to the second floor, a shadow stepped out in front of her. Grace jumped in the air just as she had that first morning when she'd whipped the covers from Meg's bed.

Jane laid a hand on Grace's arm and put a finger to her lips.

"Look out for yourself."

Then Jane disappeared into the darkness. Grace stood like a statue in the hallway, trying to catch her breath.

CHAPTER THIRTY

Grace slipped through Meg's bedroom door and hurled herself onto the bed.

"His name is Andy!" Meg blurted out. "He finally noticed me!"

"What? Huh?"

"*Huh?* Didn't we talk about not saying 'huh?'"

"I'm sorry," said Grace, wrapping her robe around her. "I ran into Jane in the hallway just now."

"You are looking a bit pale," said Meg. "But never mind all that. I have *big news.*" Meg had barely been able to get through supper with her mother, so excited was she to tell Grace what had happened that day. "He introduced himself. At school today! His full name is Andrew. Andrew James Montgomery. Doesn't that sound regal? And he invited us to his twenty-first birthday party. It's going to be a gala affair, maybe the event of the season. Grace, you know I've been over the moon about this young man for weeks and weeks. And today he finally spoke to me!"

"What did you say? He invited *us?*"

"He invited you as well," said Meg.

"He doesn't even know me. Why would he invite your maid?"

"Well... he doesn't know you're our maid. I told him you were my cousin — my cousin from Boston. Now you'll have a place to wear one of those exquisite gowns you have."

Grace stared at Meg in horror, her face as white as a sheet. "Are you mad? It's one thing to play dress-up and make-believe with you… but I am not going to do it in a room full of rich people."

"You'll be fine, Grace. You'll be perfect. Please don't worry about it."

But Grace was worried. That night she slunk back to her room with a heavy heart. *How could Meg have put me on the spot like this, without even asking me first? What on earth was she thinking? Of course I'm not going. I will not make a fool of myself.*

Having made what she thought was the only rational decision, Grace was able to set this ridiculous idea aside and allow sleep to overtake her. That night she dreamed she was alone in a garden. She was wearing a pale yellow crepe-de-chine gown with a deep lace collar; it had been one of Meg's favorites and now it belonged to her. She slowly turned to see that the garden was full of pink flowers, all shapes and sizes. In the distance she could hear voices, but she could not make out what they were saying.

The following evening, Meg worked on a strategy. From the time she was a small girl, she had always gotten her own way, and she was not about to be thwarted. What she wanted more than anything was to share the most exciting thing that had ever happened to her — an invitation from the young man with whom she'd fallen in love — with her best friend. Meg had never had a best friend before; she'd had friends and acquaintances, but she'd never known another girl with whom she felt completely comfortable. She'd never known anyone like

Grace.

It was from Grace that Meg had discovered the joy of sharing. This was something that she, an only child, had never had to do before. Her every want and need had been provided; she'd even been allowed to go to college, which was unusual. At the time, few women attended university. Most were encouraged to marry and start families, regardless of their social status. But Meg enjoyed reading, and her parents could not refuse her wish to study literature at the local university.

The same skills of persuasion that Meg had used on her parents she now employed with Grace. She would not give up until she had convinced her best friend to join her at Andy's birthday party. Besides, she had just read George Bernard Shaw's new play, *Pygmalion*. The parallels were stunning: Grace the chambermaid was the diamond-in-the-rough to Meg's Henry Higgins. In the three years they'd known each other, Meg had witnessed a startling transformation in her friend, a transformation for which she was responsible. She was proud. More than anything, she wanted to show off her creation.

If Grace wasn't certain that she was ready to make her debut in society, Meg was absolutely positive. She had groomed this girl herself. She had watched Grace adopt her every mannerism; she had taught her how to dress and style her hair… Her student had the keys: good posture, clear diction and, thanks to Meg, a wardrobe full of fashionable clothes and shoes. What more did she need?

What more indeed…

"I don't think I can do this," said Grace when she joined Meg in her room for their nightly rendezvous.

Grace had no idea how to make conversation. For the past three years, the only lengthy conversation she had made had been with Meg! And although Meg was a gifted conversationalist, there was a huge difference between chatting in a girl's bedroom and making small talk in a room full of wealthy, educated strangers.

Meg counseled Grace that less was more; the less she said, the more intrigued people would be.

"People love nothing better than to talk about themselves," said Meg. "All you need to do is smile and nod and occasionally murmur, 'Yes, yes,' or 'Oh, my, really?' You really don't have to say much of anything. Let them do the talking."

"Well... I just... I mean..."

Meg jumped off the bed and ran to her closet. She pulled out two evening gowns and handed one to Grace. "Come on, let's practice."

Grace was always delighted to play dress-up. Within minutes the girls were twirling around the room.

"Just remember, Grace, you play me better than I do."

CHAPTER THIRTY-ONE

The logistics had been nerve-wracking, but after maneuvers worthy of a five-star general, Meg had managed to get both herself and Grace to the Montgomery home, an immense Victorian mansion whose gables and cornices loomed over all the other houses in the neighborhood. Thank heaven Andy had sent a driver to pick them up. Grace had tiptoed down the servants stairs in her stocking feet, clutching her satin pumps, and quickly put on her shoes before she raced around the outside of the Browning house to join Meg in the Montgomery's Oldsmobile brougham.

"Would you try to relax and enjoy yourself?" Meg whispered to her friend. Grace was holding onto Meg's hand so tightly it was starting to go numb. She had been overwhelmed the moment she set eyes on the mansion, and became even more so when she and Meg stepped into the enormous foyer, where they were greeted by a white-jacketed butler. The butler bowed, took their wraps and ushered them into the main parlor. One of the guests was playing a Mozart gavotte on the grand piano. Grace had never seen so many beautifully dressed people all in one place. She clutched Meg's hand even tighter as they made their way through the crowd.

"See? It isn't just our clothing," whispered Meg to Grace.

Heads were turning as they passed and Grace experienced an odd sensation, one she'd never felt before. "Enjoy it, my dear. You are being admired!"

As liveried servants moved quietly among the guests, offering drinks and *hors d'oeuvres* from polished silver trays, another guest arrived. The butler greeted the handsome gentleman by name as he handed over his topcoat. He cut a dashing figure as he stood for a moment in the center of the arched entryway to the grand parlor, surveying the room. Yes, the crème de la crème of Pittsburgh society had all assembled to celebrate his friend Andy Montgomery's twenty-first birthday. He either knew or was acquainted with almost everyone in that luxuriously appointed room.

And then he noticed them.

Stunning, he thought to himself. He felt suspended in time, lost in the vision before him. Two young ladies stood at the other side of the parlor, one auburn-haired, the other pale blonde. Aside from beauty, he thought, there was something different about them – a certain studied ease, confidence and poise he had never before encountered. He couldn't quite put his finger on it. All he knew was that he had to meet them.

He stepped down the two steps into the grand parlor and snatched a glass of champagne from the tray of a passing waiter, determined to make his way through the crowd. The quest was going to take longer than he'd planned: being well-known and well-liked among this elite crowd, the young man had to stop and exchange greetings with nearly everyone in his path.

"Good evening, Mr. Mayor," he said, shaking hands with the

stately gentleman in full tuxedo who peered at him over wire-rimmed glasses.

"Mrs. Magee, how lovely you look this evening," he said as he gently took the lady's hand and kissed it. The mayor's wife blushed.

"Hello... Good evening.... How nice to see you...."

Like an eighteenth-century courtier, he would execute a slight bow as he took a lady's gloved hand and touch the back of it to his lips, reducing her to a blushing schoolgirl. The men, too, delighted in exchanging hearty handshakes with the gallant young man. He deliberately tried to keep each conversation brief without being rude, the whole time keeping his eye on the two young ladies.

"All right, Grace, you may let go of my hand now," said Meg softly. "You do look absolutely ravishing tonight, if I do say so myself. I knew that gown was perfect for you," she added, pushing a small strand of Grace's hair back into place.

Grace forced a nervous smile. Her gown was extraordinary, almost a perfect match for her slate-blue eyes – silk jacquard trimmed in ivory lace that complimented her creamy, flawless complexion. Her hair, the color of summer wheat, was swept back and twisted to one side, topped off with an exquisite jeweled hair comb. A single strand of pearls – a gift from Meg, "for good luck" – glowed around her neck with a soft radiance. Grace, at nineteen, had never looked lovelier.

Meg's gown provided an eye-catching contrast to Grace's. It had been, perhaps, a deliberate choice on her part, to highlight her friend's beauty by choosing a copper colored silk chiffon that, when they stood next to each other, made the blue of Grace's gown seem even bluer. Around the waist, Meg had tied a simple satin ribbon shot through with threads of gold silk. Like Grace's gown, it looked like a Paris original, distinctly simple and elegant.

The two young women and their style that spoke of an effortless sophistication were the envy of all the other ladies who by comparison looked like overtrussed turkeys with their bustles, ruffles, flounces and bows. Meg knew it. Grace had no idea.

"If it makes you feel any better, Grace, I'm a little bit nervous, too... just remember..."

Meg raised her chin ever so slightly. It was their secret sign to give each other a boost of confidence. Grace finally let go of Meg's hand, looked directly into Meg's eyes, and raised her chin, too. Then they exchanged a grin.

Suddenly Andy Montgomery was standing next to Meg. "Have I told you how beautiful you look tonight?"

Meg smiled flirtatiously. "Yes, I do believe you have. But please continue." She squeezed his arm.

Grace hadn't moved from Meg's side since they had arrived, but seeing how enthralled her friend was to be with the young man she had been talking about with such hope and passion, she turned away and started to look around the room at the beauty of the décor, the furnishings, flower arrangements and the paintings on the walls. Looking towards the entrance, she noticed the grand foyer for the first time. *How did I not notice? We must have come through there when we arrived.*

Her eyes moved to the enormous round wooden table in the center of the foyer, its legs carved with lions and cherubs. On top of the table sat a large ornate urn filled with fragrant white lilies and yellow roses the size of grapefruits. Her eyes swept from the marble floor to the curved banister of the staircase, and from there to the flickering sparkles of light from the enormous chandelier that hung high above the foyer like stars on a dark night.

With guests still arriving through the open front doors, the cool summer breeze made the crystals dance and tinkle like tiny bells. The piano faded away, and so did the laughter and party chatter. Grace's mind drifted. Suddenly she was listening to the soft sweet sounds of the wind chimes her Poppa had hung outside her bedroom window. He had told her that the sound it made was that of angels watching over her, keeping her safe. Grace wondered where those angels had been all these years. Maybe they had finally returned to protect her.

A peaceful calm enveloped her and she heard her father's voice – deep and comforting – say "Hello." Just as his face was about to come into focus, Grace turned to face the gentleman who had finally reached his destination.

"Hello," he repeated softly. "Your friends seem to have abandoned you. Forgive me for not waiting for a proper introduction. My name is John Haibach."

CHAPTER THIRTY-TWO

Grace found herself staring at the most handsome man she had ever seen. For a moment she had no idea where she was, or even who she was; she felt as though her mind had abandoned her body. But this man's eyes captivated her — they seemed to look right into her soul — and she couldn't turn away.

"I'm John," he repeated and he stretched out his hand, palm up, hoping she would offer hers in return.

Faced with a brand new, completely unfamiliar social situation, Grace looked to Meg for help, but her friend was across the room and out of reach, surrounded by her college friends and clinging to the arm of Andy Montgomery. Thankfully, her wits returned and as she turned to face the young man, she lifted her chin ever so slightly. That little movement worked its magic: Grace suddenly felt confident and composed.

"Grace. Grace Dodson. How do you do?" she replied, extending her gloved hand.

"How do you do, Miss Dodson," said John. He raised her hand and touched the back of her glove to his lips.

"It is a pleasure to meet you," said Grace.

"The pleasure is all mine," replied John. He noticed that she did not blush like the other young girls he had met. She merely nodded and smiled and looked him directly in the eye.

"Are you new to the area, Miss Dodson?" asked John, putting the emphasis on the "Miss" and hoping she would not correct his assumption.

"Well, not really. I..." Grace hesitated. "I moved here almost two years ago. I am from Boston originally."

She was amazed how easily the fabrication tumbled out. Emboldened, she continued, her voice becoming stronger and surer. "I'm now living here in Pittsburgh with my aunt." She nodded in Meg's direction.

"She's your *aunt?*" asked John.

"Oh, no," Grace laughed softly. "Meg, I mean Margaret, is my cousin."

This part she *had* rehearsed with Meg during their late night dress rehearsals.

"Oh," said John, sounding slightly relieved. "Is your family here as well, or do they still reside in Boston?"

"Neither, I'm afraid," said Grace. She paused and looked down at the richly carpeted floor. "My parents are no longer with us." Grace lowered her voice to a whisper, "Which is what brought me here to live with my aunt and cousin..." Again she bowed her head: *too painful to talk about.*

"I'm so sorry," he said quickly. "Please accept my sincerest condolences." There was an awkward silence. "I hope you're finding Pittsburgh to your liking," he said in a cheerier voice. "I'm from Erie myself."

The warm glow left Grace's cheeks as the hair rose on the back of her neck. Before she could formulate a reply she heard Andy Montgomery shout, "John!"

Grace and John turned to see Andy holding Meg firmly by the hand, threading their way through the other guests. "Meg, I want you to meet John Haibach, my closest and dearest friend. We've known each other since we were this high." Andy held out his hand to the level of his knee. "John," he continued, "I see you've already met Grace. Well, meet Meg, I mean Margaret, Margaret Browning."

John extended a hand toward Meg. "It's a pleasure to make your acquaintance, Miss Browning."

"Didn't I tell you she was beautiful?" Andy beamed. Meg smiled and blushed.

Grace was swimming in relief that they were no longer talking about Erie.

"Is your mother by any chance Millicent Browning?" asked John.

"Why, yes she is. Do you know my mother?" Meg sounded surprised; her mother had never mentioned the Haibachs.

"I have met her, yes, but I don't know her well, I'm afraid," John replied. A few years earlier, he'd been introduced to Mrs. Browning by his father during a business trip to Pittsburgh. He remembered not liking the woman.

"You're lucky," quipped Meg.

John smiled. How right she was; mother and daughter could not have been more different from each other. He had an extraordinary memory for names and faces, and could also recall entire conversations verbatim. He recalled the stodgy, pompous way Mrs. Browning had addressed him and his father, and he was delighted the daughter was so very much the opposite.

"It's a pleasure to meet you, Mr. Haibach," said Meg. "And do call me Meg."

"Please call me John."

Turning towards Grace, Meg added, "Grace is my cousin."

"Yes," said John. "I've been shamelessly imposing myself upon Miss Dodson. It must be difficult to have two such beautiful ladies living in the same house."

Meg beamed and Grace's cheeks turned a little more pink.

"Miss Dodson, may I interest you in a glass of champagne?" asked John. He gallantly held out his arm.

"Why, that would be lovely, Mr. Haibach." Picking up the cue from Meg, she added, "And you must call me Grace." She exchanged a knowing smile with Meg as she rested her hand on John's arm.

The switch was tripped. Grace never dreamed this opportunity to try out her new persona would yield such glorious fruit. John Haibach, the willing audience, was there to receive her as she sprang fully formed into society. He noticed that she didn't giggle, blush or flirt; she seems to have been programmed differently from all the other girls. If only he knew! She looked like the real article; she spoke and moved and gestured like the real article; she had all the attributes of a well brought up young lady from a wealthy family. All Meg's training had paid off; Grace had made that all-important first impression.

CHAPTER THIRTY-THREE

The next morning Grace was back in her maid's uniform, preparing to serve coffee in the Brownings' dining room. The whole situation seemed surreal... the night before she had been almost a debutante. And now she was Mary Dodson again, just a servant. She smiled to herself, remembering what Meg had said to her after they'd come home from Andy Montgomery's birthday party.

"I think we're both headed down the aisle!"

Meg had been sitting at her vanity, brushing her hair while Grace lay on her stomach across Meg's bed. The girls should have been exhausted, but sleep was the furthest thing from their minds – they were both lost in the afterglow of their enchanted evening.

"What?" Grace propped herself up on her elbows. "Now I know you're crazy. This was only your first date. You don't even know him yet!"

"I know all I need to know," replied Meg. She brushed her thick auburn hair up into a twist on top of her head and then let it fall about her shoulders. "I know how he makes me feel, and I know how I feel just to be near him."

Grace rolled her eyes, but tried to smile and humor her best and only friend.

"Now I know his family," Meg continued, "and I know his best friend and his best friend's girlfriend." She turned away from the mirror to give Grace a broad wink. "Besides, Andy and I think alike. What else is there to know?"

"A great deal, I should think!" Grace sat straight up on the bed to emphasize her point.

Meg just looked at her and smiled.

"Oh, what do I know?" asked Grace, slumping back onto the coverlet.

"Look who's talking," said Meg. "I saw the way you gazed at John. And – more importantly – the way he admired you. Don't deny it!"

"That's silly. You're jumping to conclusions." But Grace had to admit that, as absurd as it sounded, she was also enjoying the fantasy. She couldn't stop thinking about the handsome face that had been so close to hers just a few hours ago, those dark eyes and that dazzling smile.

She shook herself. "Well. As for John, I've only just met him. Besides, he can probably have any girl he wants, and probably does. Just look at him."

"As a matter of fact," replied Meg, "he's single and there's no one special in his life."

"How do you know that?"

"I asked, of course. And let me rephrase that: there *was* no one special in his life. Judging by the way he monopolized you all evening, I doubt he would want any other girl on his arm."

Grace leaned back and drew in a deep breath. "Do you really

think so? Do you really think he thinks of me in that way?"

"We were at the same party, weren't we?" asked Meg, a little archly.

"But what would he want with me?" Grace was already preparing herself for disappointment.

"Now who's being silly? Come here." Meg pulled her up off the bed and led her to the vanity. "Sit down." She stood behind Grace and lifted her thick blonde hair up off her neck, twisting it into a chignon. "What gentleman in his right mind wouldn't want a beauty like that on his arm? As his girlfriend, his fiancée, his wife... the mother of his children?"

For a moment the two young women stared at their reflections in the mirror. Meg was smiling; she had already seen the future.

"Aren't you getting a little ahead of yourself? He may think otherwise when he finds out I'm just a common maid," said Grace. She was not smiling.

"There is *nothing* common about you. And why does he have to know? You were brilliant tonight. No one would have a clue you weren't born into affluence like the rest of us. Even I was impressed... and maybe a little envious."

"It was fun and it was frightening. But Meg, it isn't *real.* Tonight was simply an elaborate game of dress-up."

"It was real, Grace," Meg replied sternly. "You want to forget your past? Then create a new one and move on."

Grace searched her friend's cool green eyes for some rational explanation. What Meg was proposing was beyond her wildest imaginings. No... what Meg was proposing was impossible.

Meg pressed on. "John Haibach can be more than a dream or a game of dress-up. Give him a chance to get to know you, 'my dear cousin from Boston.' He'll fall, if he hasn't already. Tonight was just the beginning. You'll see. I know these things."

"Then what do I say if he asks what I do all day? I certainly can't tell him I clean and dust and make beds!"

"Tell him you study privately, have a passion for painting, and you help your dear old aunt with her charity work."

Grace burst out laughing. How easy it was for Meg to make these things up! She always seemed to have all the answers at her fingertips.

"I'm serious, Grace."

The two stared at their reflections again and when Grace looked into her own blue eyes in the mirror, something had changed. For the first time in her life she saw possibilities she never thought existed. *Create a past and move on.*

"So... will you be my maid of honor?" asked Meg with a devilish grin.

That next morning, in the Brownings' dining room, Grace caught her reflection in the large silver serving tray and dared to smile at the image of Mary Dodson in the gray servant's uniform with the white collar, hair pinned back under a simple white cap.

CHAPTER THIRTY-FOUR

Grace had just finished arranging the breakfast platters and fine china according to Mrs. Browning's meticulous instructions, each plate positioned "just so." No plate or platter could be too close or too far from any other plate or platter, and each serving utensil had to be placed at a forty-five degree angle on the outer right-hand edge of the platter. Grace had mastered the execution of her employer's specifications on the first day she'd been promoted from upstairs maid to downstairs maid.

"I'll have my coffee now, please."

Grace was startled to see Meg enter the dining room. Usually her mother was the first to sit down to breakfast. The girls studiously avoided eye contact, even though there was no one else in the room.

"Yes, miss?" replied Grace. She was acutely aware of breaking protocol: Mrs. Browning was always to be served first, and she hoped Meg wasn't planning on antagonizing her mother.

"A cup of coffee, if you please," repeated Meg as she seated herself at the table and placed a serviette in her lap. She hadn't gotten a wink of sleep the night before and was too excited to stay in her room. Meg had come down to breakfast before her mother only once before, on the day her father took ill.

Meg's euphoria was so great, Grace could tell she was ready to throw caution to the wind. She spun around to look at Grace but just as she opened her mouth, Mrs. Browning entered the room. Grace saw the daunting matron first and dropped a serving spoon to warn her friend.

"Oh! Good morning, Mother," said Meg.

Grace picked up the spoon and retreated to the kitchen.

Mrs. Browning appeared shocked and a little upset to see her daughter sitting with a steaming cup of coffee already at her place. "Is it, Margaret?" she asked in a shrill voice. She seated herself and arranged the folds of her dress. "Am I late?" she asked, rather indignantly.

"No, I was early, Mother. I didn't sleep well last evening," said Meg.

Mrs. Browning opened her linen serviette with a snap and placed it on her lap. "I didn't think I was late," she said, glaring at Meg's cup of coffee.

"It's just coffee, Mother. I needed it to help me wake up." Meg was determined not to let her mother spoil this glorious morning.

From inside the kitchen, Grace overheard the exchange between mother and daughter. Mrs. Browning had many old-school habits from what Meg called "the Dark Ages." The daily breakfast ritual was absolutely critical to proper living, according to the lady of the house. Not only did she demand perfection in the food and the service, everyone had to be in the dining room on time. The hour never varied. Mrs. Browning believed that breakfast was the best time of day for meaningful family communication. Meg had told Grace several times that if she missed the morning ritual, she would suffer the wrath of her mother's bad mood for the rest of the day.

Fortuitously, communication between mother and daughter had vastly improved since Grace had taken over serving the morning meal. The truth was, Meg had discovered a way to communicate with Grace by conversing with, or *through* her mother. Mrs. Browning was none the wiser; in fact, she was secretly delighted that her daughter had become so much more talkative. For her part, Grace learned about the family's schedule, day-to-day routine, friends, acquaintances, etiquette, style and manners, simply by being in the room.

"Mary!" Mrs. Browning barked.

In a flash, Grace returned to the dining room.

"Remove that stale cup of coffee and bring my daughter a fresh one. Then we can begin breakfast properly together."

Grace promptly removed Meg's china cup, even though the coffee was still steaming hot. She poured a fresh cup and then served one to Mrs. Browning. The morning ritual was back on track, all the ruffled feathers smoothed back into place.

"Tell me about your evening, dear," said Mrs. Browning as she spooned a portion from the bowl of fresh raspberries and strawberries.

"It was absolutely divine," said Meg. She couldn't contain her excitement, even in front of her mother. "It was the loveliest soirée I have ever attended."

"I have never been to the Montgomerys' home myself, but I have heard it is quite exquisite. They do have the largest house in all of the Allegheny West, you know. Do tell, Margaret... I want to hear every detail." She paused dramatically, then added, "I trust that the evening was properly chaperoned...?"

"Yes, Mother, it was."

"Well, are you going to tell me about your evening or not? I don't know why I have to pull everything out of you, Margaret. Can't you just for once simply tell me without my having to pry every detail from you? Who was lucky enough to make the guest list, aside from you, my dear?"

If that woman would just be quiet for a moment, thought Grace as she freshened the coffee cups and served strips of bacon, taking care not to catch Meg's eye. It was really all she could do to keep a straight face.

"Mr. and Mrs. Montgomery were both there," said Meg, taking a small bite of bacon. "As were the Mayor and Mrs. Magee." She knew that would impress her mother.

"I knew I should have gone with you," declared Mrs. Browning. "Did you ask him about his revitalization plans, or about the new cultural center?"

The blank look on Meg's face told Mrs. Browning that her daughter had not discussed civic matters with the Mayor. "So how was the young Master Montgomery?" She was hoping her daughter's encounter with the heir had proven promising.

"Well, let's just say I hope to see him again," Meg replied simply.

"Oh, this is great news, Margaret," her mother exclaimed. Mrs. Browning had been pointing out acceptable young men to her daughter ever since the girl had turned sixteen, hoping she would marry "up." The Montgomerys far exceeded her expectations. "Who else was there? Don't make me pull every name out of you."

"Well," Meg hesitated ever so slightly, toying with her mother's eagerness and ambition and letting the suspense build. "Do you know a John Haibach? From Erie?"

This she tossed out deliberately for Grace's benefit.

"Haibach? Yes," said Mrs. Browning. "I do remember meeting a Haibach, but his name was Lawrence or Lorenz. They are in the meatpacking business, I believe. Actually, one of the larger companies."

"Yes," said Meg. "John remembered meeting you on a business trip with his father once."

Mrs. Browning was flattered. "Really? I do remember him now. Very handsome, if I recall correctly."

"John or the father?"

"John," replied her mother. "Well, his father was, too. Is he single?"

"John or his father?" Meg asked, knowing where her mother's mind was heading.

"Oh, *Mahhhhgaret!*"

"His father is deceased, Mother, and yes, John *is* single and very handsome," Meg added, again for Grace's sake.

"All I'm saying is that he, too, would be a fine suitor for you, dear – as a second choice, if the Montgomery boy doesn't work out."

Grace deliberately let a serving spoon clang loudly against a platter.

CHAPTER THIRTY-FIVE

Grace couldn't believe she'd dropped the spoon, and yet it was something that had to be done. She had long ago gotten used to being invisible. Mrs. Browning only acknowledged her presence when she needed something and Meg did the same when her mother was there. This morning, however, more than ever Grace knew she inhabited two realities simultaneously: as Meg's friend and co-conspirator, she could make her presence known.

"I believe John Haibach already has his eye on someone, Mother," said Meg, stealing a glance in Grace's direction when she was sure her mother wasn't looking.

"Pity," replied Mrs. Browning. "One can never have too many choices. Is it anyone we know?"

"No one you know, Mother. She's a beautiful young woman from Boston."

Grace turned her back to the ladies to hide her smile, pretending to be busy with the dishes on the sideboard. Just then, the butler entered the dining room, a white envelope in his gloved hand.

"Madame, please excuse the interruption. This was just delivered. I thought it might be of importance."

Without looking up, Mrs. Browning raised her hand to receive the envelope, but the butler glided right past her and handed it to Meg.

"For me?" asked Meg.

"Yes, Mademoiselle," said the butler. Mrs. Browning still had her hand in the air.

Meg ripped open the envelope, slipped out the card and silently read the handwriting below the gold embossed initials A-J-M.

Mrs. Browning couldn't contain herself. "Well, what is it, Margaret?"

"It's an invitation to afternoon tea at the Hotel Schenley... for tomorrow," she replied, barely able to suppress her excitement. The Hotel Schenley was Pittsburgh's finest, where the city's elite gathered on Sunday afternoons to sip tea and sherry and nibble on cucumber sandwiches and petit-fours.

"From whom?"

"From Andy, Mother. It's from Andy Montgomery."

"Andy? Don't tell me he goes by a silly nickname, too... Well, read it Margaret!"

Meg stared at the handwritten invitation for a long time.

"Out loud, please!" Mrs. Browning was beyond annoyed with her daughter's lack of cooperation.

"All it says, Mother, is that he enjoyed my company last night and is inviting me to join him for tea on Sunday. And he is anxiously awaiting my reply."

"Wonderful, dear. It has been ages since I have been to tea at the Schenley. Of course you'll need a chaperone."

Meg shuddered; if her mother accompanied her, it would ruin everything.

"Oh," said Mrs. Browning, "I forgot I have our ladies' auxiliary luncheon tomorrow right after church."

Meg exhaled with relief. "We don't need a chaperone, Mother. This isn't the nineteenth century."

Mrs. Browning was too thrilled to argue. The only thing on her mind was what a wedding to a Montgomery would do for her social standing. "Let's go write your acceptance. We mustn't keep a Montgomery waiting!"

As Meg followed her mother out of the dining room, she slipped the invitation under the silver coffee carafe.

"Tell me more about the evening, my dear," said Mrs. Browning, her voice trailing away along with the rustle of her skirts. She led her daughter to the study to write a note of acceptance that would seal her future as a well-placed lady in society.

Grace saw the note when she cleared the dishes.

My dear Meg,

I can't tell you how much more enjoyable my twenty-first birthday was made by your lovely presence last evening. Thank you for sharing such a memorable celebration with me. It would be our extreme honor if you and Grace would join both John and me for high tea, this Sunday afternoon at two o'clock at the Hotel Schenley. John and I anxiously await your reply.

Warmest regards,

Andy

"You and Grace?" Heavens above! Grace was thrilled to have

been included and petrified at the same time. This game of dress-up was becoming serious.

That evening, Meg told her friend how her mother had paced the floor of the study, dictating exactly how the reply should be written. Meg pretended to write down her mother's every word but instead composed her own response, sealing the envelope before Mrs. Browning had a chance to review it.

"I wrote that you and I would be delighted to join Andy and John for tea, but it would be more convenient if we met them at the hotel."

"Oh… fine," said Grace. She was not nearly as enthusiastic about this date for High Tea as Meg was… things were moving rather too quickly.

"You should be thrilled, Grace. They both want to see us again, and tout de suite!"

"And what?"

"That's French for 'right away.' If you don't want to go for your own sake, you must at least go for mine. Besides, I've already sent our acceptance. They're expecting us both and it would be extremely improper for me to go alone. "

"Yes," Grace sighed. "I see your point."

"Oh, Grace, please don't behave as if you're being sentenced to jail."

Grace abruptly stood up, wrapped her robe tightly about her and started for the door.

"I'm sorry! What did I say? I didn't mean to offend you. Grace, please don't go… please, sit down. Please."

The look on Grace's face frightened Meg. She reached out and took her friend's hand. Grace came back and sat down on the bed.

"I apologize for reacting that way. It's just that this is really a struggle, this pretending to be someone I'm not."

"Don't be silly. You're not pretending at all. You're just being your new self. Think of it as having attended finishing school and practicing your new skills. Think of it as God's way of making up for all the bad things that happened when you were a child. You deserve a great deal of happiness, my friend."

Grace shrugged her shoulders.

"Do you think you can relax a little bit and let some happiness come to you?" asked Meg.

Grace thought about it. "I'll go with you, Meg. For you and Andy."

CHAPTER THIRTY-SIX

The Hotel Schenley was known as the Waldorf of Pittsburgh, and it was every bit as grand as its New York counterpart. Presidents William Howard Taft, Theodore Roosevelt and Woodrow Wilson had signed the register and many other rich and powerful people had stayed within its Louis XV walls and dined under its crystal chandeliers. Frequent visitors included two of the most successful Andrews in America's financial history – Mellon and Carnegie – along with George Westinghouse, A. J. Heinz, Diamond Jim Brady, Enrico Caruso and Sarah Bernhardt. Lillian Russell actually lived there: she had the entire fourth floor to herself.

Andy Montgomery and John Haibach arrived at the hotel early and settled themselves in the lobby with a clear view of the entrance. Propriety dictated they escort the two young ladies into the grand salon, rather than risk any puritanical tongue-wagging that might tarnish the girls' reputations should they enter by themselves. It was a busy Sunday at the Schenley; an endless parade of well-dressed characters passed before the two young men, including a curvaceous middle-aged woman in an enormous feathered hat. Her red velvet skirt was just a little too tight, but what made walking even more difficult for her were the five toy poodles – each on a separate leash, all of them gripped in one leather-gloved hand. Her other hand was occupied, trying to keep her hat on her head. The rambunctious poodles chased each other around her legs, wrapping their leashes around her ankles, and with each step she had to stop and twirl about and get the little dogs back into some sort of order. By the time she reached the elevator, one of the poodles got loose and made a beeline for the front door, trailing his leash behind him.

"Oh, poor little thing!" cried Grace as the white ball of fluff scampered by her, just as the doorman was swinging open the door to allow her and Meg to enter. The doorman quickly tipped his cap to the young ladies and then dashed after the fleeing dog.

"I wonder whose sweet little pet that is," said Meg as she took her friend's arm and entered the hotel lobby.

John and Andy sprang to their feet when they saw their dates arrive. The young women's entrance caught everyone's attention, and this made the boys even more proud. Grace's ensemble, a deep blue jacket in the new style which fell long over the hips, looked elegant with its wide shawl collar and tucked-seam skirt. Meg wore a similar afternoon suit in a shade of green that set off her auburn hair. Heads turned as the foursome made their way to the dining room.

While a string quartet played discreetly in the background, two separate, simultaneous conversations took place under crystal chandeliers as white-jacketed waiters brought the tea and silver multi-tiered serving trays laden with tiny sandwiches and sweet cakes. Grace was far too nervous to eat. She took a watercress sandwich and set it on the gold-trimmed china plate in front of her.

"More tea?" asked John. Not waiting for a reply, he filled her cup.

"Thank you."

"This is quite a place, isn't it?" he began. "My father brought our family here when it opened in 1898."

Grace smiled and nodded and sipped her tea.

"It was Pittsburgh's first steel-framed hotel," he went on, "the tallest ever built in this city. Did you know that U.S. Steel was born here?"

"No, I did not," said Grace. She did not know what U.S. Steel was, but found herself somehow glad to be with this handsome young man in the place of its birth. John continued to make small talk about the hotel, its history and the important people who had stayed there, and Grace continued to listen attentively, smiling and nodding, absorbing every word.

How would John ever get to know this lovely creature sitting next to him? She had hardly said a word. Was she really that shy? Or was she deliberately trying to captivate him by being silent and mysterious? She had a natural dignity; one would almost call it a solemnity, except when she smiled – a smile that transported him to heaven. Again he noticed that she didn't giggle, and this made her different from the others. The gravity of Grace's life had obliterated that giddy tic that afflicts so many young women.

"Something tells me that I just may be visiting Pittsburgh much more often from now on," he said with an encouraging smile, hoping to prompt Grace to start talking.

Grace merely returned his smile.

John decided to take a more direct approach. "So tell me about you, Gracie. I want to know everything."

Grace's eyes glazed over; the color drained from her face and her eyes filled with tears.

"Grace?" said John softly. He had no idea what he'd said but wished he could take it back.

"You called me Gracie."

"I am so sorry. That was terribly ill-mannered of me. It just slipped out. I didn't mean to sound so familiar." John felt so awful he wished for a moment that he could crawl under the table. The last thing in the world he wanted was to cause this beautiful girl distress.

"No, no, it's fine," she replied, placing her hand on his for an instant. "No one has called me Gracie since my father. I'm sorry... it may have been your voice, or the way you said it. But I'm fine... really."

John passed her the handkerchief from his pocket and she dabbed the corners of her eyes. "I'm so sorry. I won't make that mistake again, I promise," he told her.

The color returned to Grace's cheeks and she smiled at him. "I would very much like it if you *would* call me Gracie."

He looked into her blue eyes and repeated her name, "Gracie." A warm feeling washed over her, a feeling so familiar, one she believed had been lost long ago.

John steered the conversation back to topics with which he felt comfortable – *May God strike me dead if I make this beautiful girl cry again!* he thought to himself. He talked about his family and the family's meatpacking business. In an effort to impress her, he described how his grandfather had come to America with his brothers from Germany back in the 1880s, settled in Erie, and went from being simple butchers to owning their own meat market, a business which eventually grew to become one of the largest in the state. "Almost six thousand people in western Pennsylvania earn their living in meatpacking. Of course, I don't want to stay in that business forever; what I'd really like to do is work in the automobile industry."

"John?" Andy broke in. "Don't bore the hell out of her on the first date with that scandalous industry your family's involved in." Not long before, Upton Sinclair's *The Jungle* had ripped the lid off the shameful conditions in Chicago's meatpacking industry. "At least let her get a word in edgewise."

John fell silent, the wind temporarily removed from his sails. Grace knew it was now her turn; she had to talk about *herself.* She caught Meg's eye and Meg raised her chin ever so slightly.

CHAPTER THIRTY-SEVEN

"I'm an only child, born in Boston," Grace began. Now that she had no choice, the story she had barely rehearsed had to unfold. "My parents were English, and like you, I too am Catholic." She paused, hoping this would suffice, but the rapt look on John Haibach's face told her that she had to go on.

"My father was a man of many talents. He could sing and dance, and he was very artistic, very good with his hands. He could draw, paint and even sculpt. I don't think there was anything he couldn't do. He was also the kindest man I have ever known."

John smiled. "It sounds like you're his number one fan. Which of his talents did you inherit?"

"Not many, I'm afraid."

"And your mother?"

Grace paused for a moment. "My mother..." she sighed. For an instant, her memory flashed upon the image of Ida Dodson in the Brookville jail. She shut her eyes and took a deep breath. "My mother was very old-fashioned, the sort who wore lace and cameos. Everything had to be perfect in our house or life would end. She was very strict, with far too many rules and regulations. But she loved us."

She was describing Mrs. Browning, the only proper ideal of a mother she knew. And then confusion set it: *Meg and I are supposed to be related... are our mothers sisters, or our fathers brothers? Please God, don't let him ask!*

"Us?" asked John.

Grace looked up at him, her blue eyes wide with surprise.

"You said 'but she loved us.' I thought you were an only child," said John.

"Did I?" asked Grace, flustered. "I am. I meant my father and me."

"Ah," John nodded. "And what did your father do?"

Grace didn't know much about Mr. Browning; Meg had never mentioned what her father did for a living. *Where do I go from here?*

Then it came to her in a full-blown burst of inspiration: "My father and mother owned a clothiers in Boston, Beacon Place Couture. They imported women's fashions, mostly from Paris, and then duplicated and sold them here for substantially less. Few can actually afford Paris originals, unless you're a Vanderbilt, of course."

"Well, that would explain your exquisite wardrobe," said John, admiring the detail of her perfectly tailored jacket and skirt.

Grace caught Meg's knowing smile at this last exchange. Meg gave her a wink.

"So how exactly are you and Meg related?" asked John, eager to keep the conversation rolling along.

Meg saw Grace freeze and leaped into the fray. "Grace's mother and my mother were sisters."

Thank you, Meg... Safe for the moment!

Grace gave her friend a grateful smile. *Of course, Mrs. Browning was born in Boston... as long as neither John nor Andy ask her about her dear, departed sister, I'll be all right.*

Before she turned back to John, Grace noticed Meg's jacket lying beside her on the divan, the Beacon Place Couture label plainly visible. "Excuse me, Meg, you've got a few crumbs on your jacket," said Grace as she leaned over and pretended to brush at the fabric, folding the label out of view.

"Thank you, Grace," said Meg, her eyes sparkling with merriment. She gave her friend a wink.

But all this subterfuge was hard work. Grace felt herself retreating into her silent, distant place. John noticed immediately and, like a fisherman about to lose a prize catch, began talking in a most animated fashion about the fancy lady in red and her poodles, in hope of lightening Grace's mood and reeling her back in.

"That woman had no more business walking five dogs at once than I have making Parisian fashions," he declared.

"That woman," said Andy, "is Lillian Russell, the actress. She's known for being extremely eccentric."

But all Grace could think about was the poodle that had made its mad dash for freedom, practically under her feet... and how much she herself wanted to escape right now.

"So, Andy, is it wealth that makes people so peculiar and strange, or are they just that way to begin with?" asked John.

"Why are you asking me?" Andy shrugged. "I'm not peculiar or strange. You tell us, John."

"I'm neither wealthy nor peculiar," replied John, keeping his eye on Grace and hoping their banter would bring her back.

"But, if I ever get that peculiar or eccentric, do me a favor, John, just shoot me," said Andy.

"Ah," John sighed. "Something to look forward to. I shall do just that, you have my word."

The young men's laughter yanked Grace out of her reverie and she smiled at John, who was trying so hard to keep her entertained. The hour was late and guests began exiting the dining room. Meg and Andy led the way through the hotel lobby, and Grace took John's arm and followed. As they exited the hotel, they saw the doorman handing a dirty little white poodle to a bellhop.

"Please take this up to Miss Russell on the fourth floor," said the doorman.

Andy and Meg turned to see John and Grace's reaction. They all burst into laughter except for Grace. A cold shiver went up her spine as she turned to catch a final glimpse of the little dog being sent back to confinement.

CHAPTER THIRTY-EIGHT

As far as Meg Browning was concerned, matrimonial success was a foregone conclusion: she would be Mrs. Andrew Montgomery and Grace would be Mrs. John Haibach, and the logistics that would take them to this happy state were mere minor details. Of course she would think this way; with the exception of her father's death, life had never thwarted Meg. Grace, however, embarked upon a series of double dates with Meg, Andy and John, with great trepidation. She clung to Meg like a lifeline, needing her by her side for that chin-lifting boost of confidence, or to bail her out of an awkward situation.

The girls managed to slip out of the house unnoticed on Sundays, when Mrs. Browning was busy with charity functions, and often met their young men at Schenley Park, a four hundred and twenty acre expanse named for Mary Croghan Schenley, the same woman who had donated the land for the hotel.

As the foursome wandered the park's formal Roman and English gardens, Grace could not believe the vast expanse of natural beauty that surrounded her.

"John," she asked, taking his arm. "Is it true that one woman made all this possible?"

John smiled at her indulgently. "Yes, Grace. We owe all of this to Mrs. Schenley, one of the finest citizens Pittsburgh has ever had. Just wait until I show you the Phipps Conservatory and Botanical Gardens."

"I never knew there were so many different kinds of flowers in Pennsylvania!"

Her heart filled as she and John wandered wordlessly through the orchids and roses and hundreds of other varieties of flowers. She made up her mind that one day she would have a garden of her own.

It was on their third double date, when the four were strolling toward the lily pond and John was explaining the differences between Cattleya and Cymbidium, that they heard a voice calling in the distance. "Andrew, is that you?"

The two couples spun around to see a squat, top-heavy figure scudding toward them.

"Aunt Carol," said Andrew.

Grace detected a lack of enthusiasm in Andrew's greeting.

The woman was in her sixties and conservatively dressed, except for a broad-brimmed black hat topped with black feathers, three times the size of her head. Grace thought it made her look even shorter and heavier than she already was. Since her wardrobe indoctrination from Meg, she had become rather expert at judging style and proportion. This hat, she felt, made it seem as though the poor woman was trying to hang onto some semblance of her youth.

"What a surprise to see you here of all places," crowed Aunt Carol. "I didn't think you were the type to fritter away your time in a garden, Andrew. Are there no sporting events today?"

"Aunt Carol, what a pleasant surprise," replied Andy, through gritted teeth. He leaned in to give her a quick peck on the cheek.

Meg, who was holding onto Andy's arm, gave him a tug.

"Oh, forgive me. May I present Meg Browning? Meg, this is my Aunt Carol."

"It's *Mrs. Carol Horton*," said the lady, her voice rising in annoyance at her nephew's informal introduction. Meg extended her right hand but Aunt Carol did not reciprocate.

"Meg?" repeated the lady with disdain. "Surely that's not your given name, is it my dear?"

"Yes, it is," replied Meg. "Rather plebeian, but then *Andy* loves it."

Aunt Carol quickly turned her attention toward the other two. "John, it's always a pleasure to see you," she said, extending her hand, expecting the gallant kiss John Haibach always delivered. He did not disappoint.

"It is nice to see you as well, Mrs. Horton." John briefly kissed the back of her hand.

Aunt Carol seemed to melt a little. "And who have we here?" she asked, turning toward Grace.

"May I present Miss Grace Dodson? Miss Dodson, Mrs. Horton," John said with all formality. He would not make the same mistake his friend Andy had made by presenting the young woman on his arm too casually. Aunt Carol looked Grace up and down as if she were on an auction block. Grace was immediately uncomfortable, but she didn't show it.

"How do you do?" Grace smiled, politely offering her hand. "It's a pleasure to make your acquaintance, Mrs. Horton."

Aunt Carol actually took Grace's hand, but her eyes were focused on Grace's waistline. "I used to have a figure like yours, just a couple of years ago."

Meg stifled a snigger and Andy turned his face to hide the smile that threatened to turn into a laugh.

"Enjoy it while you can, my dear. It's so fleeting," said Aunt Carol, nodding her head so vigorously that her giant hat threatened to topple from her head. "Dodson? I'm not familiar with that family name. Is that D-A-W-D-S-O-N?"

Without the slightest hesitation Meg answered before Grace had a chance to think, let alone open her mouth. "Yes, it is. Grace is my cousin from Boston."

"Boston?" Aunt Carol sounded almost delighted. "I'm in Boston quite often; it is one of my favorite cities. I wouldn't be surprised if our social circles intersected. Perhaps we can visit the next time I'm there."

"Perhaps," Grace replied. There could and would be no plans made to meet up with this woman, in Boston or anyplace else. She swiftly changed the subject. "Your hat is just lovely, Mrs. Horton."

"Why, thank you, my dear." Aunt Carol adjusted the brim.

"It was very nice to run into you, Aunt Carol," said Andy. "We were just heading into the Conservatory." He gave her a peck on the cheek to signal farewell.

"Good afternoon, Andrew. Give my best to your mother. Always a delight seeing you, John," she added, giving him a schoolgirl smile. "Miss Dawdson, I'll look you up next time I'm in Boston."

With a wave of her hand, Aunt Carol toddled down the path.

Grace and Meg grinned at each other.

"I seriously hope you didn't really admire that millinery disaster!" Meg whispered in Grace's ear. "That's D-A-W-D-S-O-N," Meg added in a mocking tone. "*Do* look me up next time you're in Boston,"

The girls giggled.

The spelling change was brilliant. It would be virtually impossible to look Grace up – in Boston, Pittsburgh, or anywhere else.

CHAPTER THIRTY-NINE

As that glorious summer shifted into autumn, Grace realized that for the first time in her life, she actually looked forward to each new day. The workweek was punctuated by double dates with John, Meg and Andy, and with each date Grace grew more confident and comfortable in her new social set. As long as Meg was within view, she didn't stumble. And her feelings for John Haibach were growing stronger.

Early one September morning, while Grace was setting the breakfast table, there was a knock at the kitchen door. Jane opened the door to find a teenage boy in a messenger's uniform.

"I have a letter for Miss Grace Dawdson," said the messenger.

"We have no one here named Grace," said Jane. "You must have the wrong house."

The boy studied the envelope. "Isn't this the Browning residence?"

"Yes, but there's no one here by that name."

Jane was about to close the door when she saw Grace enter the kitchen. "Hold on a minute. Did you say Dodson?"

The messenger held the envelope in front of Jane's face.

"Mary! I think this is for you."

"Dis here's for a Grace," said the impudent messenger. "You

gotta sister?"

"Sometimes I'm called Grace," she replied. The messenger handed her the envelope and Grace stared at the spelling of her last name. *It could only be from John or Andy or perhaps – no! – old Aunt Carol.* She ripped open the envelope and read the note.

Grace didn't serve breakfast that morning. Jane sent her to her room when she saw her turn pale and clutch her stomach; perhaps the girl had received bad news from a member of her family.

"You go lie down for a bit, get some rest."

Jane's advice, of course, was overheard by one of the other servants and the news flew like lightning through the servants' grapevine. Meg learned of it from the chambermaid. She raced down the servants' stairs at the back of the house to the kitchen. Jane and Sarah jumped to attention when Meg burst in. Sarah, the newest member of the household staff, was so rattled to see Mrs. Browning's daughter out of her element that she dropped a china cup.

Meg stared at the broken pieces of porcelain scattered on the floor. "Where's Mary?"

"Sh-sh-she isn't feeling well," stammered Sarah.

"But where is she?" repeated Meg.

"I believe she's in her room, resting," said Jane.

"What's going on in here?" Meg heard her mother's voice coming from the butler's pantry – a small room that separated the formal dining room and breakfast room from the kitchen – where the fine china, silver and serving trays were stored. Panic set in and Meg darted back out of the kitchen.

Jane dropped to her knees to pick of the shards of china, just as

Mrs. Browning burst through the pantry door.

"I'm so sorry, Ma'am," said Jane. "It was an accident and completely my fault."

Mrs. Browning glared at Jane and Sarah, furious her morning routine had been disrupted over a cup. "Try to be more careful," she said as she swept back through the butler's pantry to the breakfast room.

Meg was already seated at the table. "Is something wrong, Mother?" she asked, manufacturing a surprised look.

"Mary's not feeling well, so Sarah will be serving us this morning. If she doesn't break all my fine china first, that is."

But Meg could not take her mind off Grace or the mysterious news that had upset her. It took all the strength she could muster to finish breakfast with her mother. Just before the hour was up, she excused herself.

"I have to be at the university a bit early today, Mother. Bye-bye." Before Mrs. Browning could object, Meg ran out the front door.

Moments later she slipped back into the house through the rear kitchen door and tiptoed down the back stairs to the servants' quarters, the part of her home where she didn't belong. She stopped at the bottom of the stairs and stared down the bleak hallway at the row of closed doors.

Suddenly one of the doors opened and Jane stepped into the hallway. Meg forced a sheepish grin.

"You're taking chances," said Jane in a low voice. "I'll warn you if somebody comes, but I'd be quick if I were you."

Meg rapped softly on the third door. There was no answer.

She rapped again and slowly opened the door. There was no one inside. Meg stepped in and looked around. The servants' rooms had seemed so much bigger when she was a little girl who sneaked down the back stairs to go "exploring." Meg made a circle around the tiny room, running her fingers over the bed, the little chest of drawers and the boxes piled in the corner marked "for charity." And then she noticed, on the back of the door, the slate blue gown swinging gently on its hanger – the gown Grace had worn to Andy Montgomery's birthday party. Meg felt a lump in her throat.

CHAPTER FORTY

"Mary, are you feeling better?"

Grace had tried to slip back into the house unnoticed, but Jane heard the squeaky floorboard on the way to the servants' stairs.

"Yes. Thank you, Jane," said Grace.

"You caused quite a stir this morning, you did," added Jane, not unkindly. "But I'll let Meg tell you about it. She's waiting for you... in your room."

Grace hurried down the back stairs to find Meg sitting on her bed.

"Grace, are you all right? What's going on? Where were you?"

"What are you doing here? Are you crazy?" answered Grace. "You're going to get us both in trouble."

For a long moment, the girls searched each other's faces for explanations.

"I went for a long walk," Grace began. "To think. I'm not really sick. Well, maybe I am. I don't know what I am, or what I'm doing, or what I'm feeling." She pulled the envelope from her coat pocket. "This came this morning."

When Meg saw the envelope was addressed to Miss Grace Dawdson, she knew it had to be from John. "How was this delivered?

Who accepted it?"

"It came by messenger; he brought it to the back door. When Jane heard it was for Grace Dawdson, she assumed it was for me."

"Thank goodness for Jane!" said Meg. "If that messenger had talked to Mother, you *never* would have gotten this." She pulled the note from its envelope. "I should have anticipated this. I'm sorry I didn't think things through very well. But don't worry about Jane. She's on our side."

As Meg read the note a big smile spread over her face and she began to bounce up and down on the bed. "This is great news! He wants you to come to Erie next weekend and meet his mother!"

Grace said nothing; she hardly felt like bouncing with exuberance.

"Obviously, his mother's opinion is important to him, Grace. You know what this means, don't you?"

"What?"

"Well, you don't invite just anyone to meet your mother. I may never let Andy meet *my* mother."

Grace stared at the floor as the significance of John's invitation slowly dawned on her and shook her head. Meg lifted Grace's chin and looked her in the eye. "We've had this conversation a hundred times, Grace."

"I know, but I don't think I can do this," she whispered. "I'm not you. I can't pass myself off as something I'm not – not with John's family."

Meg took both of her friend's hands in hers. "Stop thinking of it that way. You're not passing yourself off; you are entering your new life. Listen: my mother has stepped on and over many people in her life to climb up the social ladder. It's what people do. With you, Grace, it was simply fate that took the step for you. And you are every bit as good a person – if not better – than my mother or me. Style and class is in your blood, and destiny is finally making things work for you. It's your turn now. So enjoy it!"

Grace smiled and squeezed Meg's hand, and her eyes filled with tears. Meg's voice cracked; blinking back her own tears, she told her friend, "You have taught me more than anyone in my entire life. I don't know what I would be like if you hadn't shown up when you did. I was a spoiled little rich girl with a grudge against life, and you made me realize there is so much more than the amount of money you have or your social class or what you wear. I'm a better person for having known you, Grace. Or should I say Grace Dawdson Haibach!"

The girls embraced and wiped away their tears. "Now, you *are* accepting this invitation. You'll go to Erie and meet his mother, be your gorgeous, gracious self, and they, too, will fall in love with you, just as John did."

"I can't go to Erie, Meg. Not without you."

Meg laughed. "Well, it would be a little awkward for me to accompany you to meet John's mother. How would we explain that?"

Grace shrugged her shoulders and shook her head. "I don't know," she said sadly.

"You'll be *fine*, Grace. Just remember, if you get stuck, raise your chin and pretend you're me. It's what you've been doing all along, isn't it?"

There was a soft knock at the door, Jane's warning that Mrs.

Browning was on her way to the kitchen.

"Speaking of your mother, what am I going to tell her about going to Erie?"

Meg jumped up and headed for the door. "I have to go before Mother catches me down here. We'll think of something, Mrs. John Haibach... I promise." She gave Grace a triumphant smile and then dashed down the hall, up the stairs and through the kitchen to the back door. There, on the floor just next to the door, lay her satchel of schoolbooks. She had left them on the table in the foyer when she'd rushed out of the breakfast room. Meg silently thanked her ally. If her mother had found them, she would have gone on a rampage looking for her. *That Jane, she thinks of everything.*

Grace remained in her room, her eyes closed tight and her hands clasped in front of her face. She tried to concentrate on the sound of her breath, her chest rising and falling as she took in bigger and bigger inhalations. Little by little, a sense of calm enveloped her as she realized she was praying without words. She pictured Meg, her best friend, the only best friend she'd ever had, boarding a train to Erie, her head held high, her smile pleasant and confident, as if this were something she did all the time. Without fear. And then Meg's face turned into Grace's, and Grace saw herself going forward, with confidence and self-assurance.

She remembered the night she left the O'Malleys for the Erie railroad depot and her determination to control her fate. Only this time she was not a desperate sixteen year old who would have done anything not to go back to the orphanage.

I'm going... I'm doing this... I can't not go.

CHAPTER FORTY-ONE

Grace did go to Erie to see John Haibach and meet his family, and at the end of that beautiful weekend, her beloved had asked her to marry him.

That Monday morning at the park, when she and John looked out on Presque Isle, Grace had heard what he said, and yet it felt as if he'd said it in a foreign language, a language she'd just begun to learn. She had to translate each word in her head before she understood the meaning of the question. And then her heart began to fill with joy, but still she could not speak.

John mistook her hesitation. "I'm sorry. I suppose I should have asked your aunt's permission first. But I didn't know if it was appropriate."

Grace's brain was slow to re-engage. She just stared into his dark eyes and traced the outline of his strong jaw with her eyes, settling on his smile, which hadn't changed.

I need to say something now, she told herself.

"That isn't necessary. She isn't my legal guardian."

John let out an almost audible sigh of relief. "We had better get going," he said, checking his watch. "I don't want you to miss your train."

On the way to the station, John talked a mile a minute. He had planned everything. They would marry in Erie at St. Mary's Church, the family parish. Grace would have to move to Erie so that she could begin making the wedding arrangements along with his family. He had already decided upon where she was to live, both before and after the wedding. Grace realized that John Haibach was a man who knew what he wanted: he had formulated a plan and its means of execution down to the smallest detail.

Grace's head was swimming:

What shall I tell my employer?

How will I explain I have no money of my own?

How will I tell him my last name is really Dodson, not Dawdson?

How would she ever be able to keep her past in the past? The risk of marrying into a well-known and affluent family was enormous. Someone was bound to recognize her; some small detail would surface; people would put two and two together and this whole new wonderful life would come crashing down.

But he loves me, and I love him. And it would be wonderful to feel part of a family again.

Great possibilities began to flood her mind. She would no longer be a maid. She would never again have to make up someone else's bed, never again have to be subservient to the whims of wealthy people who didn't care a fig about her. She would be Mrs. John Haibach, the envy of many.

Not bad for a poor orphan girl.

When they arrived at Erie Station, John looked at Grace with a puzzled expression on his face. She had not said one word on the whole drive.

"You never answered me," he said. "Gracie, would you consider marrying me?"

Grace looked him straight in the eye. "*Consider* marrying you? No," she said, her face deliberately bland. Then she broke into a mischievous grin. "I will *definitely* marry you. Yes!"

And just in case he hadn't heard her the first time, she said it again.

"Yes!"

John sighed with relief and his smile exploded like fireworks on the Fourth of July.

As the porters grabbed the luggage, John took Grace by the arm. "Are you sure you'll be all right?" he asked.

With John on her arm, how could Grace be anything but all right? She still could not get over the sense of enormous care and protection that emanated from this handsome man who guided her up the steps to the first class car, signaling the porter to follow with her bags.

"Yes, of course I'll be all right. This isn't my first train ride, you know," she replied with a smile.

John laughed and brought his face close to hers. She wanted to kiss him right then and there, in front of the porter and the other passengers, but John spoke first.

"And it won't be your last, my dearest. There are so many fantastic places I want to take you." He squeezed her hand and kissed her gently on the lips. "I'll come down to Pittsburgh to see you just as soon as I can."

The porter settled her bags in her compartment and took out

his handkerchief to brush at an invisible spot on the window ledge. "Is there anything else you require, Madam?"

This man's job is to see that I'm comfortable, she thought to herself. *I think I could quickly become accustomed to people taking care of me!*

"Thank you, no, I'm just fine," said Grace as she seated herself and smoothed her skirt. John Haibach's proposal of marriage still rang in her head, and she replayed every moment of that morning. The bright green park where she and John had sat on the bench, very close to one another, closer than she had ever sat with anyone before. The trees that shaded the bench bent and whispered with the breeze, as if they too were offering encouragement. Sitting next to John made her feel safe, as if she would never, ever come to harm again.

In her mind's eye, she saw the sun shimmering over the water, the lake rippling as the colors changed with the warming day. Presque Isle had looked almost colorless when they first sat down, but had blossomed with pink and gold as John talked about this favorite place. She heard his voice, deep and soothing. He loved explaining things; everything was brand new information and she soaked it all up like a sponge. John Haibach was thorough, too, the way he had figured out every step the two of them would take, right up to the wedding and afterwards. The happiness she had felt at the moment she told him, "Yes!" That feeling had far outweighed the fear. She saw his face before her and his enormous smile when he finally heard her answer, "Yes!"

Yes, thought Grace. That one simple word was all it took to make him happy.

The train was leaving the rail yard, rolling through Erie; as it cleared the edge of town it rolled a little faster. Grace sank into blissful fantasy, imagining herself as Mrs. John Haibach, the two of them making a perfect home with fine furniture and draperies and a modern kitchen, a home where she would have a maid to make up the beds and keep everything tidy. Maybe one day they would have a family and her life would be complete, in perfect order.

Then apprehension began to set in. *What if I make some dreadful mistake? What was that word Meg used?* Faux pas. *What if I take a false step?* The stakes were much higher now that the brass ring was within her reach. She had committed to memory the made-up story of her parents and her Boston background after she divulged the details to John and his mother. But what would happen if he ever found out about her real family?

Grace shook her head vigorously as if to dislodge the idea. Her family no longer existed, she told herself. Her father and mother were probably still in prison. For all she knew, they might both be dead. Her two brothers were dead; Lord only knew where her sisters had ended up, or if they were even still alive. But what if they *were* alive? What if one day, as Grace and John were walking about in Erie, they should be approached by a woman who resembled her... "Gracie, is that you? It's me, Linnie!" How could she explain that?

She looked out the window and watched the countryside flashing by. It looked as beautiful as it had when she'd taken that train to Erie a few days ago. As she listened to the rhythmic chuff-chuff-chuff of the locomotive, Grace wondered how much more practice it would take for her to feel completely comfortable in this new world.

And yet, after Mrs. Haibach had grilled her with a thousand

questions, the formidable woman had accepted her. *I passed muster*, Grace said to herself. Amazing! And it felt so good to be accepted by John's family.

The train was picking up speed, the scenery rushing by faster and faster. Grace's mind raced ahead to her next concern. *The Haibachs are well known and well-connected in Erie*, she thought. *What if they know one of the well-to-do families who took me in as a foster child? What if they know the people who ran St. Joseph's Orphan Asylum?* John's mother, Mary Haibach, was a strong Catholic and probably the sort of woman who made big contributions to her church. What if she wanted to see where her money went? What if she paid a visit to the Mother Superior, and one thing led to another, and the Mother Superior happened to mention one particularly difficult orphan by the name of...

"Stop it, stop it, stop it!"

Grace looked around to see if anyone had heard her. But, of course, no one had. She was all by herself in a first class compartment, surprised at the sound of her own voice. She dug in her purse and pulled out the pink carnation. It was dry and faded, but still held a hint of the delicious fragrance that made her think of John and the new family she was about to join.

If my sisters are dead, there is no threat to my future happiness. But I can't know for sure, and I'll have no peace until I find out what happened to them.

Suddenly she sat up straight. *I don't have to wait for them to find me.*

She raised her chin, her eyes clear and focused on the far distance, on a place where she would not have to be a victim of circumstance.

I will find them first.

CHAPTER FORTY-TWO

"Mary gave notice this afternoon," Mrs. Browning announced, as soon as Meg had seated herself at the dining table. "She will be here through the end of the month, and she'll be training Sarah to take over the breakfast service." This was the most essential item in Mrs. Browning's mind: there would be no interruption to the household routine.

Meg did not react to the news. She unfolded her serviette, placed it in her lap, and took a sip of water.

"I guess Mary's trip to Erie had less to do with a sick relative and more to do with her fiancé," Mrs. Browning continued, a bit more loudly.

Meg already knew – Grace had told her of John's proposal the night before when she'd returned from Erie – but feigned ignorance, chiefly to annoy her mother. She served herself a small portion from the platter of roast chicken and then looked up at her mother with an expression of mild interest.

"Did you hear what I said, Margaret? At least someone in this house has found a husband. *Mary* is getting married!"

Meg widened her eyes in mock surprise.

"I gave her a few extra dollars," said Mrs. Browning in a self-satisfied tone. "I'm sure it will come in handy. They're just starting out and it can't be easy on a tradesman's salary. I also gave her a letter of recommendation, in case she has to continue working. After all, she *is* an excellent maid."

It was all Meg could do not to burst out laughing.

"What? You were about to say something?" her mother snapped.

"Nothing, Mother," Meg replied. Grace wouldn't be needing either money or a job. "What makes you think she's marrying a tradesman, Mother?"

"She's a *maid*, Margaret. A good one, but still, a maid."

"Speaking of getting married, Mother…" Meg held up her left hand. A large diamond engagement ring sparkled on her ring finger. "So am I."

As Meg had predicted on the night of Andy Montgomery's birthday party, she and Grace were both on their way down the aisle. The fact that they'd both become engaged over the same weekend was a topic of long, giddy conversations for many late nights after Grace's return from Erie. Meg was positive the two young men had planned the whole thing with marvelous optimism and synchronicity.

The questions that had haunted Grace before she gave John her answer – *What shall I tell my employer? How will I explain I have no money of my own? How will I tell him my last name is really Dodson, not Dawdson?* – no longer seemed like obstacles.

"Your mother was most gracious to me when I gave notice. And generous," Grace told her friend. "It was more than a few dollars she gave me."

Meg was surprised and pleased. "Maybe my mother is more

human that I give her credit for. She did tell me she thought you were an excellent maid."

Grace burst out laughing. "Well, I am sure your mother must be so relieved her prayers have been answered: her daughter is marrying a Montgomery!"

"Yes, yes! She was only upset that Andy hadn't asked her permission first."

Grace was even more thankful that John hadn't asked Mrs. Browning's permission either. The wedding date was set for the summer of the following year, but the planning had already begun and her betrothed was doing most of it. As soon as Grace had agreed to marry him, John began making arrangements for her to move to Erie, renting a large apartment near the family home, which Grace would share with his twin sisters, Loretta and Florence. The sisters were delighted at the prospect of moving out from under Mama Haibach's watchful eye, and Grace was glad she'd have congenial roommates.

But even with all this to look forward to, Grace was reluctant to make the move. The Browning house had become her home – the first real home she'd had since she was three.

"I'm having the wardrobe trunks brought up from the basement for you," said Meg one night as Grace's moving day was drawing near.

"What for? I don't need all those trunks," said Grace.

"I think you do," replied Meg. "You will *not* be sending all your clothes to Erie in boxes marked 'For Charity!'"

Grace hadn't thought of that.

That night, after Grace had gone back to her room and turned down the bedclothes, she heard a knock on her door.

"May I come in?" asked Jane. "I just wanted to congratulate you and –"

Grace opened the door wide and ushered her in. "Why thank you, Jane. That is very kind of you."

Jane glanced at all the boxes and clothes that filled Grace's tiny room. "I wanted to wish you well. You will be very much missed."

She dug her hand into the pocket of her robe and pulled out a small package wrapped in tissue paper.

"This belonged to my mother. She gave it to me when I left Ireland and came to America. For a better life."

Jane put the parcel in Grace's hand. "Open it."

The tissue paper fell to the floor. It was a gold compact engraved with curlicues and flowers.

"Oh, Jane, this is beautiful! But this was your mother's. I simply cannot accept it!"

"Yes, you can," said Jane. "I insist. Since you've been living here, I've watched you change and I've watched the change in Meg. Whatever happened between you two girls was almost like a miracle. You've both grown up to be fine ladies. Real ladies. Perhaps my mother thought this little thing would help me become a lady when I got to Pittsburgh. I want you to look in the mirror now and then, and be proud of what you see."

Jane snapped open the compact and held the little round mirror up to Grace's face. "I'd like to think you've gotten to a place not many of us get to go."

Grace's eyes filled with tears.

"There, there," said Jane. She put her arms around Grace's shoulders and gave her a gentle hug. "You just carry on. For all of us."

The following night, Meg helped Grace fold and pack her beautiful, scarcely-worn wardrobe. Some of the clothes had never been worn at all – at least not by Grace. Others, like the slate blue silk gown, were imbued with special memories. The girls wrapped each pair of shoes in tissue paper before placing them, heel to toe, in the bottom of the trunks.

"I think the shoemaker did a marvelous job," said Meg, examining the lining of a patent kid lace-up walking shoe. "Do you find them comfortable?"

"Oh, yes! Much better than wadded-up newspaper," replied Grace, as she wrapped the other shoe in tissue.

"Do you think I should throw in a few yardsticks? Just in case you forget how to walk like a lady?" Meg chuckled.

"I will miss living here," replied Grace, her face turning melancholy. "I'll miss our nightly chats. I'll miss *you*."

Meg took her friend by the shoulders and gave her a little shake.

"Now, now, dear girl... After all my hard work, I would be insulted if you wanted to continue living below stairs!"

She snapped the lid closed on the trunk and fastened the buckles. "Besides, we'll be seeing each other soon enough... at your wedding, Grace Haibach."

CHAPTER FORTY-THREE

Grace, betrothed, moved to Erie to start her new life. The battered old door on Mary Dodson, house servant, slammed shut, and deluxe double doors swung open as she settled into the spacious apartment that John Haibach had rented for her and her future sisters-in-law.

John had done well, selecting a building that had every amenity three young women could desire. Florence and Loretta embraced the newest member of their family with a fondness that Grace found lovely and unsettling at the same time. Little by little, she began to enjoy her new family. While his sisters fussed over their new home and new roommate, John decided to show his fiancée the best parts of Erie. Now that they were officially engaged, they could finally enjoy some time alone with each other, and they spent as much time together as John's business schedule would allow.

They took evening strolls through the park, often ending up at a bistro for an aperitif or cup of hot chocolate. On Saturday mornings they walked along the lake, where John would point out the different kinds of boats that plied the busy waterway. He loved watching the joyful expression on her face as he showed her the places he was most proud of in his hometown. He also loved to show her off at society functions and charity events, and he could never get over how her beauty cast a spell upon all who met her.

Grace clung to his arm the evening he took her to the Art Gallery in Erie's new public library on Perry Square. The square was named for Commodore Oliver Hazard Perry, who commanded the U.S. Naval fleet in the Battle of Lake Erie. As John and Grace walked through the square, he went into a detailed description of the War of 1812, proud to show off his knowledge of local history. Then he stopped himself. "Oh, listen to me go on. You probably learned all about that in school."

No, she thought to herself; *the sisters at St. Joseph's Orphan Asylum had had very little to say about American history. They were more intent upon catechism and thrashing us with a ruler when we didn't give the right answers.*

But Grace didn't want him to know how little she knew of history. "Oh, please go on," she said, giving his arm a little squeeze. "It's so much more interesting to hear you explain it."

Inside the library John proudly introduced his fiancée to Mrs. Card-Catlin, the Erie grand dame who had founded the art gallery.

"I am so glad you both could be here," said the great lady. "We have a new Constable over there." She gestured with a long-gloved hand. "No doubt you both will tell me that it is the most fabulous painting you ever saw."

John and Grace weaved through the crowd of well-dressed art patrons to a large oil painting, a landscape. John studied the canvas with a thoughtful expression on his face. Grace stood quietly beside him, trying to mimic his pose. But she didn't know what she was supposed to find in the picture. It was a lovely scene, full of dark green trees and a sweeping meadow. But to her, it didn't look any better than the Pennsylvania countryside or the forested county of her youth.

John broke the silence. "So, my dear, was Mrs. Card-Catlin right? Is it fabulous?"

Grace shrugged her shoulders. "I'm not sure," she replied. "I've seen more lovely landscapes right outside my window, when I took the train to Erie."

John slipped his arm around her waist, delighted with her answer. "I quite agree. Shall we look at a few more paintings, as long as we're here?"

"If you wish," replied Grace. Somehow, she could not put much enthusiasm into her voice.

"Then, let's go," said John decisively. "This isn't my cup of tea either. Besides, we'd enjoy ourselves much more having a walk around the square."

Grace was relieved. She didn't know much about art, nor did she think standing around in front of oil paintings was how she wanted to spend time with her fiancé.

The next night, John presented Grace with a better idea: tickets to the Erie Philharmonic. Once again, the couple found themselves back in Perry Square, the center of Erie's arts and culture. They paused in front of the concert call. A man in a black suit and top hat stood on the sidewalk, playing a violin. Grace could see a few coins sitting at the bottom of the open violin case which lay at the violinist's feet; he was playing a lively tune with great virtuosity, and a small crowd began to gather around him.

"Oh, my," Grace whispered. "Are the concerts held right here in the street?"

John stared at her. "Are you joking with me, my dear?"

She looked up at him, wide-eyed. He chuckled. "Yes, my love. This is the before-concert concert. This fine musician is just giving us a taste of what awaits us inside."

A few of the onlookers laughed good-naturedly at John's remark.

"Why, this is all quite wonderful," Grace exclaimed. The violinist finished his performance with a flourish and tipped his hat in her direction as people applauded.

Tossing a few coins into the open violin case, John led her up the stairs to the concert hall. Grace was utterly captivated by the sumptuous décor. She had never been in a theater before. She looked closely at the other patrons, well-dressed men and ladies, most of whom were older than she, scanning for faces that might recognize her own. She couldn't help it; as much as she wanted to relax and enjoy being with John, her old fears were rekindled when they went out in public together.

They found their seats and John took her hand in his, patting it gently. "You know, our Erie Philharmonic orchestra is every bit as good as your Boston Symphony Orchestra. At least, people who know about these things have told me that ours measures up to the best."

"Oh, really?" Grace replied, not knowing what else to say.

"I'm sure you'll tell me when the concert's over if you think our orchestra is as good as Boston's."

"I'm afraid I wouldn't be able to tell you that," Grace replied.

"I've never been to the Boston Symphony."

John's face registered surprise, but before he could say anything more, the conductor tapped his baton and raised his arms. Suddenly the violins, violas and cello swooped into Haydn's *Symphonie No. 39.* Grace studied the violinists, looking for the man who had been playing outside on the sidewalk. Failing to find him, she let her thoughts drift as the orchestra worked its magic.

The melody was unfamiliar; the only music she'd ever heard were the hymns enforced by Mother Superior and the waltzes Meg had sung when they were playing dress-up and dancing around Meg's bedroom. She glanced over at John; his eyes were closed and he seemed to be deeply entranced, with a smile on his lips. Grace decided to do the same. She closed her eyes and lost herself in the music.

When the symphony was over, Grace and John remained in their seats while the other patrons filed out of the hall.

"Well, Gracie? Did you enjoy it?"

"Oh, yes," she beamed. "What a wonderful new experience!"

John studied her face for a moment. "I just cannot believe that you've never been to a symphony or an art gallery before you came to Erie."

Grace paused for a moment, collecting her thoughts. "Well, I guess I was just too preoccupied with helping my parents when I was younger; I hardly ever went out."

Just as John Haibach had promised the love of his life that there would be many more pink carnations, he told her he'd make sure that she would never want for symphonies or art galleries or any other uplifting cultural experience.

"John," Grace said, her mouth set. "It would be all right if you didn't show me all the art galleries."

John laughed. "That's all right with me, Gracie. I'm not much for paintings either! But I was just wondering…" He took her hand, bringing his face close to hers.

"Yes?" Grace looked up at him.

"Well, I was thinking it would be nice to have a string quartet play for our wedding reception."

"That's a wonderful idea!"

"So, my love, would you prefer Haydn or Purcell? My mother favors Johann Sebastian Bach, but I must confess I find his music a bit too strident."

"Strident," Grace repeated. She had not encountered this word before but it sounded like something she wouldn't want to have at her wedding reception. At last she spoke. "Haydn… he wouldn't be strident, would he?"

John threw his head back and laughed. "You're a funny one, Gracie. And I adore you for that. Haydn will do just fine and no, he won't be strident, I promise you."

CHAPTER FORTY-FOUR

Although Grace was surrounded by familial comfort, happiness and new cultural experiences, anxiety continued to plague her. Perhaps it was the fact that she was enjoying life for the first time; perhaps it was the feeling that she didn't deserve any of this. She found herself thinking about her family, and she lay awake at night wondering what had happened to Linnie.

Did she go to a good home, a loving family? Was she as happy as I? Did she still like to play hide and go seek?

She couldn't banish the thoughts from her mind. With only a couple months to go before the wedding, she decided she had to do something to put these nagging questions to rest. Someone at the orphanage had once mentioned that Linnie had been adopted by a family in Oil City, a small town on the Allegheny River not far south of Erie. Grace decided that her only chance to get any information about her sister was to write a letter to *The Derrick*, the local Oil City newspaper.

To her utter shock, the paper printed a public notice:

Grace Dodson, of Erie, writes the Derrick for assistance in learning the present address of her sister, Linnie Dodson. "They were inmates of an orphan asylum," she writes, but neglects to designate it by name, and they were separated 12 years ago. Miss Dodson had been informed that her sister was taken to Oil City. Any information will be thankfully received by the Erie sister, whose address is Grace Dodson, No. 1716 Sassafras Street, Erie.

She spent a few more sleepless nights worrying that someone would see the notice and put two and two together, even though she was now known in Erie as Grace Dawdson. She hadn't dared put the name of St. Joseph's in her letter to the newspaper. Well, if some busybody did put two and two together, she would cross that bridge when she had to. There were only so many things she could worry about at one time.

Two weeks later, a letter addressed to Grace Dodson arrived at the apartment.

Dear Grace,

Strange that I should find you now. Two days ago I located our brother Jimmy...

Could this be true? Did Linnie not know that Jimmy had died at the orphanage?

Grace read on in disbelief. Linnie described how she had actually found Jimmy, how she had told a girlfriend where she worked that she'd once had a sister named Grace and a little brother named Jimmy and how they'd all been separated at the orphanage. The girlfriend had an aunt in Oil City who had adopted a little boy from Erie about that same time and his name was Jimmy. The girlfriend would occasionally see them both at Sunday Mass. That next Sunday, Linnie went to her friend's church and the moment she saw the boy –

now seventeen – she knew without a doubt it was Jimmy, *her* Jimmy.

But, Linnie wrote, she had decided not to approach her brother. "Why bring up a past that wasn't worth remembering?"

Grace now made it her habit to intercept the postman at the front door every day. She and Linnie exchanged a few more letters before they made plans to meet in person – a meeting Grace insisted should take place in Oil City. Not only did she want to see her sister, she was determined to see for herself this boy her sister *swore* was their brother. Telling the Haibachs she had to visit an old family friend, Grace made the journey by bus to the boarding house where her sister lived.

"Gracie?" Linnie stared at the well-dressed young woman standing in her doorway.

"Linnie," her sister replied, stepping forward and graciously extending a gloved hand. Linnie repressed an impulse to embrace her; there was something about her formal bearing and beautifully tailored traveling suit that did not invite hugs and kisses. Instead, she took Grace's hand in both of hers and held it. Grace looked into her sister's eyes and smiled.

"It is so good to see you. You're looking very well."

Linnie giggled and waved a hand. "C'mon in, sit down."

Grace followed her sister into the sparsely furnished room. There was a small sofa covered in faded chintz, an armchair covered in a different fabric, and a small table and chair that probably served for eating meals and letter-writing. Linnie caught her sister looking about the room.

"I bet you're wondering where the bed is," she laughed, a little self-consciously. She strode over to the closet and flung it open. "Murphy bed!" she declared.

The Dodson girls had lived very different lives since they'd been separated. Linnie had been adopted into a loving family when she was six years old. Her adoptive parents had been good to her, although her father had been placed in an insane asylum just a few years earlier due to "mental problems." Her mother worked as a caterer and Linnie worked as a bookkeeper at the railroad station. This, she explained to Grace, was how she had met her husband-to-be. "He's a wonderful man, Gracie, and he's got a good job. He's a brakeman for the railroad!"

While Linnie talked, Grace studied her face.

Yes, she bears a slight resemblance to me, Grace thought, *but if I met her on the street, I would never guess she was my sister.* Linnie's hair was neither cut nor styled; she wore it in a braid that went halfway down the back of her shirtmaker dress.

Grace's update was brief. She told her sister only that she had never been adopted and that, at sixteen, she had run away to Pittsburgh where she'd found a job as a maid. But now she was back in Erie and she, too, was about to be married – also to a wonderful man.

"Well, isn't that sumpin! Both of us, about to get married!"

Grace smiled and nodded. It was strange: two sisters, close in age, with nary a trait in common, other than impending weddings. Their conversation ground to a halt. Grace decided to tell her sister about their older brother Will, and his death at the age of fifteen at

Father Baker's Home for Boys. This was followed by another long silence. Then Linnie told Grace that she'd made contact with their oldest sister Rhoda, who lived in Sewickley Township, south of their childhood home, and was married to a coal miner with three children of her own.

"Becka's married, too. She's doin' fine."

It all seemed so long ago. Listening to her sister's updates on her long-lost family, Grace realized that too much time had gone by; the strong bond she had imagined, the longings and fantasies that had haunted her dreams, had no more hold on her. These people were almost strangers to her.

It wasn't until conversation turned to memories of the orphanage that Grace and her sister found an emotional connection.

"I din't want to leave," said Linnie. "I cried and cried. Even wished I could go back. I din't want to leave you and Jimmy."

"Well," said Grace, patting her sister's hand, "We didn't have much say in the matter. The worst atrocity was the Mother Superior lying to me, telling me that Jimmy had died."

"Why'd they do such a mean thing?"

Grace shrugged her shoulders. "Who knows why they did half the things they did?"

"I am so sorry you were stuck there all that time."

Grace managed a smile. "It's all in the past and that's where it shall stay. We've all survived and moved on to better places… most of us," she added, thinking of Will.

Linnie nodded sadly. "I will never forget that beatin' I got. And I din't do nothin' to deserve it."

"The scratched bench?" Grace asked reluctantly, not wanting to hear the story again.

Linnie shook her head violently as she recalled the time one of the nuns beat her with a stick until bleeding welts rose on the backs of her legs – all because another orphan had accused her of scratching the varnish on a brand new wooden bench. Nobody bothered to investigate; Linnie was just yanked into the hall and beaten to within an inch of her life. Her eyes filled with tears at the memory. "What a horrible place that was."

Grace remained stoic; she had survived many incidents just like this one and with far worse consequences. She would not allow them to resurface, not now.

"Enough of the past," said Grace. "It was a lifetime ago. Shall we go see Jimmy?"

CHAPTER FORTY-FIVE

The sisters stood across the street from the National Hotel and stared at the entrance for the longest time.

"Why don't we just go inside?" suggested Grace. "We're bound to see him. We could even have lunch."

"Oh, no, Gracie. That kinda place is too ritzy for folks like us, even if we could afford it."

Grace would gladly have paid for their lunch, but she didn't want Linnie to feel uncomfortable; she remembered how awkward she'd felt the first time she visited the Hotel Schenley. She let the matter go.

Finally a car pulled up in front of the hotel, and a tall, good-looking bellboy came out to help with the luggage. Grace recognized him right away.

"It *is* Jimmy!" she whispered to Linnie.

"'Course it is!" Linnie whispered back.

Grace was overcome with joy and relief to see her baby brother, all grown up and such a handsome young man to boot. She grabbed her sister by the hand. "Come, let's see if he recognizes us!"

Before Linnie could protest, Grace hurried her across the street to the hotel, where Jimmy was unloading suitcases onto a cart. Grace wasn't sure what she was going to say; she just wanted a closer look *and* she wanted her brother to see his long-lost sisters.

"Excuse me," said Grace, stepping close to the young man. "Can you tell us where the post office is?"

The bellboy looked up with a strange expression on his face. Grace was certain he recognized her.

He stared at Grace, then at Linnie, and at Grace again; then, pointing to the building next to the hotel, he went back to loading the luggage cart.

The sisters looked to see a huge sign jutting out over the sidewalk: United States Post Office, Oil City. When they turned back to speak to Jimmy, he was halfway through the hotel door, pushing the luggage cart.

Linnie grabbed Grace's hand.

"'Where's the post office?' You asked him *where's the post office?*"

Grace felt like an idiot. The sisters walked away from the hotel and down the street past the post office. Then Linnie started to laugh, and soon Grace was laughing too. However, they both were disappointed their brother hadn't recognized them.

"But why would he?" asked Grace. "He was only three when we last saw each other. I know *I've* changed."

"Well, that's sure a fact," replied Linnie.

That afternoon, Grace returned to Erie with brighter spirits and a new outlook. Not only had she found her sister Linnie, she'd found the brother whom she'd long believed dead to be alive and well. She resolved to send him money every month, in a plain envelope addressed to James Dodson, care of the National Hotel, Oil City,

Pennsylvania, with no note and no return address. It made her smile every time she tucked a five-dollar bill into the envelope. *Perhaps he thinks he has a secret admirer,* she thought to herself. In 1913, five dollars was an entire week's salary.

She could rest easier knowing her other sisters, Rhoda and Rebecca, had survived their escape out the back window of the Dodson cabin. At last Grace was ready to move on. The nightmares stopped. Her love for John grew stronger with every passing day, and she was finally able to take an interest in the wedding preparations.

Then, two weeks before the wedding day, a letter arrived.

"They spelled your name wrong," said Florence, who had met the postman at the door. She handed Grace the envelope. It was indeed addressed to Miss Grace Dodson, not Dawdson.

Oh dear, what now?

With great apprehension, she opened the envelope and pulled out a card: it was a hand-drawn picture, in different colored inks, of two hands shaking in friendship. One hand was obviously a man's, the other a woman's; both were surrounded by roses. Under the hands was written "Gracie Dodson," and to the right of the hands, a laurel wreath encircled a poem:

The leaves

are green,

Likewise the vine.

And I have chosen you

for a friend of mine.

Chosen you from

all the rest,

Hoping you
May prove the best.

Grace flipped the card over but the reverse side was blank. There was neither a signature nor a return address on the envelope. She stared at the drawing, trying to make sense of it. There was something vaguely familiar about the roses and the printing. And then it came to her: the wooden blocks her father had made for her when she was three. The colors and the style of the artwork were identical to those wooden blocks.

Grace walked past Florence through the parlor and headed straight for her room.

"Good news or bad?" Florence called after her.

"Just a congratulations card from an old friend," Grace replied, trying to make her voice sound offhand.

Grace went into her bedroom and shut the door as a flood of memories and questions swept over her.

Is he out of prison? Where is he living? Why is he contacting me now? What does the card mean? Obviously he's reaching out, but why and why now? How did he even find me?

Then she remembered the engagement announcement that had appeared in all the local newspapers. She was, after all, marrying into one of the most well-known and influential families in Erie.

But how did he know it was me? All the announcements spelled my name D-a-w-d-s-o-n, and said I was from Boston. Perhaps that's why he didn't write anything on the card... just in case it wasn't me. He took a chance that I would know it was from him. What in heaven's name do I do now?

218

Grace's mind was racing, and sleep eluded her that night. The next morning she visited the local Erie post office to inquire about the postmark.

The postmaster told her the letter was mailed from a rural post office that operated inside a general store in a small township called Richardsville, not far from where she was born. Grace went straight to the train station and bought a ticket to Richardsville. She would go to this general store/post office the next morning to inquire if anyone knew the whereabouts of her father. Then she would pay him a visit.

CHAPTER FORTY-SIX

Having a plan helped to calm her anxiety. It had been over eighteen years since Grace had seen her father. She knew that if she found him, it would not be the same experience as finding Linnie and Jimmy. This was not something she wanted to do, but something she *had* to do. She had to know what her father wanted from her.

With the hand-drawn card in her purse, Grace boarded the train and traveled back to the deep woodlands of Pennsylvania. She told the Haibachs she needed to visit Meg in Pittsburgh; her best friend was also making wedding plans and needed her advice. Grace smiled ruefully at the silliness of her excuse – *as if I could give* Meg *advice!*

After a five-hour train trip and a short carriage ride, Grace found herself in front of the Richardsville General Store, a rustic, two-story building with a small sign in front that said Richardsville Township Post Office. A cowbell clanged loudly when she opened the front door. On every side were dry and canned goods, tackle, feed for livestock – the store was so crammed there was barely room to move around. For a moment, Grace was reminded of the Vernors' general store in Wattsburg, where, as a child, she'd worked for a couple of weeks before getting sick on the ladder. Except this store was smaller, dustier and much more disorganized. She wondered how customers or the proprietor could find anything.

Across the room, a teenage girl sat on a stool behind the counter, sound asleep. Grace cleared her throat loudly, but the girl remained slumped on her stool, snoring, her head on her chest.

"Pardon me," said Grace in a clear voice. There was no response.

"Pardon me, miss," Grace tried again, a little louder. The sleeping girl was oblivious. Grace was about to reach across the counter and give the girl a gentle shake when she was startled by a deep voice behind her.

"Kin I help you?"

She spun around to see an old man standing by the door. His hands were clasped in front of him and he smiled politely. "Kin I help... Gracie?"

How does he know my name?

Grace glared at the man; he was very thin and wore a tattered old plaid shirt, well-worn wool pants held up by suspenders, and an old pair of scuffed black work boots. She searched his wrinkled face and deep-set eyes for a clue to his identity.

Suddenly they were startled by a thud, followed by a groan. Their heads snapped toward the counter just as the teenage girl pulled herself up off the floor. She peeked over the counter, saw she was not alone, and, smiling sheepishly, clamored back up onto the stool.

"Silly girl, you're s'posed to be watchin' the store," the old man growled. "Can't even stay awake. Geez!"

"Sorry," the girl mumbled. "Can I help you?"

The old man turned toward Grace. "Don't mind her. She's

'bout as useless as a chocolate teapot. I'll take care of this one. This here's Gracie. This is my daughter," he announced proudly.

Grace felt like she had been punched in the stomach. *Could this be my Poppa?* She stared at the old man, searching his face for some glimmer from the past, something she could recognize, as his deep voice continued to resonate through her head. *This here's Gracie. This is my daughter.*

Perhaps it was the way he said her name, or his tone of voice, but suddenly there it was: the deep, calming voice – the touchstone she had been looking for. But she hadn't expected it to happen this way; she didn't think she would find him right at the first stop.

"You got my card, I guess. I know'd it was you I read 'bout in the papers. I know'd it instantly. So how's my special little girl?"

That did it. It was true: it *was* William Dodson standing before her. A tiny corner of her heart began to melt, just a little. But then her father moved toward her, arms open wide to give her a hug, and Grace stepped back out of reach. She wasn't ready for such close contact… not after so many years.

"Come, Gracie, let's go upstairs. I'll make us some tea and we'll catch up," he said, gesturing toward the stairs. "This is my store. I live upstairs." His voice held a hint of pride.

Grace followed him upstairs, without having uttered a single word to this man who was her father.

William Dodson's sitting room was small and cramped and cluttered, just like his store. He had to remove things from the chairs before they could sit down. Grace, like the lady she had become, removed her gloves and used them to dust the seat before she sat.

Her father made a pot of tea and talked and talked. It was difficult for Grace to listen; thoughts filled her mind, crowding out his voice. Once upon a time, all she had ever wanted was to be safe in his arms; now the man sitting across from her was a total stranger.

"We was released early for good behavior, me and your Uncle Frank," said William Dodson. "Weren't too bad, seven outta twelve years."

Grace quickly did the math. *Twelve. I was only twelve when you were released. And I was still in my prison. Why didn't you come for me, if I was your special little girl?*

"After I got out, I wandered around some, tried to find work here and there. Tried to find you children, too."

Well, you didn't try hard enough. She wanted to lash out at him, to tell him about the hell *she* had lived through, had grown up with, and had learned to endure in silence. It would make penitentiary life seem tame. But she couldn't bring herself to say any of this out loud.

My life is perfect now, she reminded herself as she looked around the confined, untidy space where her father lived. *Would my life have really been better if he* had *come for me?*

Grace sighed with relief as she heard her father mention Rebecca's name. As it turned out, a local blacksmith and his wife had taken her in after she had escaped from the Dodson cabin and raised her as their own. She was the only one that William Dodson had been able to locate after his release from prison, and she and her husband had been gracious enough to take him in.

"I stayed with them three, maybe four years, 'til I opened this store," he said.

Hearing that made Grace feel a little better – at least some members of her family had found kinship after all the terrible events that had blown the family apart. When there was a lull in the conversation, Grace filled him in on the family members she had found – Linnie, Jimmy and Rhoda – and she told him about Will. Her father had never learned the fate of his oldest son until now. He displayed no emotion; he only nodded.

How had they all become so numb toward one another?

CHAPTER FORTY-SEVEN

Grace looked out the window and checked her watch. She had seen and heard enough, and she wanted to catch the Erie-bound train before dark.

As she began putting on her gloves, her father said, "So, Gracie, how've you been? Judging your appearance and those mighty fine-looking clothes, I'd say you've done real good for yourself. According to the papers, you're quite a lady, marrying yourself a rich one."

Grace's insides turned to ice. Here it comes, she thought. *Now I'll find out what he wants from me.*

She gave her father a steady look, saying nothing.

"Well, good for you, Gracie! That well-to-do family from Boston that adopted you did a mighty fine job raising you. Probably better than I could've done."

Grace was dumbfounded. *He thinks I was adopted into a wealthy family.* She started to set him straight, but then thought better of it. *Let him think whatever he wants. Just tell me what you want from me and let me get out of here.*

William Dodson seemed to read the thoughts that crossed his daughter's face.

"I don't want nothing from you, Gracie. I just wanted to wish

225

my special little girl a happy life."

Grace wasn't entirely convinced her father wanted nothing from her; she sensed there was something more he wanted to say, but she wanted this visit to end. They had spent a little over an hour together, carving out an awkward exchange that resolved nothing and only widened the distance between them.

"I really must be going," she said, as she stood up and smoothed her skirt.

"Oh!" William jumped to his feet. "Do you have to rush off? I can make us a bite to eat. You hungry?"

"No, thank you, I really must go. It's a long train ride back to Erie."

She walked to the staircase that led down to the store, her father trailing behind her. As her foot landed on the first step, she felt her father's hand on her shoulder. His touch sent a chill down her spine.

"Gracie?"

She turned to look at her father's hand; he quickly lifted it.

"Gracie, I'm sorry," he whispered.

This caught her off guard. *What exactly was he sorry for? Sorry for destroying their family? Sorry they were orphans? Sorry for not coming to rescue her from the orphanage? Sorry for what?* She was not expecting any kind of apology from him, but it did open a door. Now was the time to ask.

"Did you and Uncle Frank murder that man?"

William Dodson appeared stunned by the question, as if it had just dawned on him that all this time, his own children might have thought he was guilty.

He looked deep into his daughter's eyes and his voice was firm. "No, Gracie."

She acknowledged his answer with a small nod. In that moment she knew in her heart that he was innocent, and that what he was sorry for was… everything.

"I'm sorry, too," she replied as she headed down the stairs.

"I'll take you to the train station," he said as he followed her back into the store. Grace's Poppa had hoped to spend more time with his special little girl.

"No, thank you. That won't be necessary." Grace was ready for this visit to be over now – even if it meant walking several miles back to the train station.

"Well, I'm gonna anyway, and that's that," her father replied.

"No, really, I'm quite capable –"

"I go right by the station on my way home," the young girl behind the counter piped up. "I can take her, if I can leave a little early today?"

"That would be perfect, thank you!" Grace answered quickly, before her father had a chance to offer an alternative.

"Fine, Flo, you take her," sighed William. "At least you're good for something besides sleeping on the job."

Flo, now wide awake and full of energy, jumped off her stool and rushed out the door to untie her horse and buggy. Grace and her father stood awkwardly on the front porch.

"Sure been nice seeing you, Gracie."

"Yes, you, too." Grace put on her gloves and extended a hand. She did not want him to try to hug her again. Father and daughter shook hands, as if closing a business deal, and Grace walked out to the waiting horse and buggy.

"Say, Gracie!" her father called. "Did your legs ever get straight?"

Grace looked back at him and smiled. She lifted up her skirt to just above the ankles, confident that from a distance he would not see the real yet subtle truth – that the heel of the right shoe, like all her right shoes, had been fitted with a lift.

"Yes, they did."

Those were the last words she ever spoke to her father. It was the last time she ever saw him.

The moment Grace and Flo headed off down the road, she regretted not walking. Instead of the quiet ride she had hoped for, Flo came to life. She announced that she would take them on a scenic shortcut to the station, and began to prattle on without taking a breath.

"...my worthless husband up and left me just before my babies were born. Twin girls, they're on to five years now. My folks said I drove the bastard away, but I didn't have nothing to do with him leaving. Now I don't talk to them anymore either, my folks. It's just me and my babies, and that ain't been easy..."

Grace tried desperately to tune her out. She needed to think, to sort through the maelstrom of thoughts and emotions and feelings that had come unburied. She tried to recall every word her father said to her and relive every awkward moment. She wished she could go back, start the whole encounter over, this time more prepared. There was so much more she wanted to say to him, to ask him.

"...I been so danged tired, my babies came down with mumps

a couple nights ago, so I been up with them for two days now. That's why I been so drowsy at the store. Your poppa been a lifesaver, giving me this job and all. I don't know…"

The word "Poppa" brought Grace out of her own head with a violent shudder. She turned to glare at Flo.

"Do I talk too much?" asked the girl.

"I'm sorry to hear your girls are sick," Grace replied. "And yes, you do talk too much."

Flo shrugged. "Well, I ain't got nobody to talk to. Not even your poppa will talk to me."

My poppa. Grace cringed. *Would this ride never end?* She turned her body away from the chattering girl and tried to look at the scenery. It was the most beautiful woodlands she had ever seen. The silly girl was right: this short cut really was the scenic route. Grace took a deep breath as she was overcome with a sense of *déjà vu.* In the distance, over the tops of the hickory, white oak and maple trees she saw the top of an old cabin.

"Turn right!" she exclaimed, pointing to a dirt road just up ahead. "There, up there!"

"Why?" asked Flo. "Nobody uses that road no more, not fer years."

"Do you mind?" Grace pleaded.

Flo gave in and they continued down the dirt road a few hundred yards.

"Stop!" Off to the side of the road, Grace could see a narrow path, shrouded by weeds and shrubbery that lead to an old, dilapidated cabin.

"I don't think no one lives there no more, Miss... not fer some time," said Flo.

Grace nodded. "I'll be right back." She jumped down from the buggy and swiftly headed up the path.

"Suit yourself," Flo called. "I'll just get me some shut-eye while I wait."

At the end of the path Grace found herself under a huge maple tree. She looked up through its graceful branches at the blue sky beyond and watched the leaves dancing in the gentle breeze. She patted the trunk of the old tree.

"Hello, old friend," she whispered.

The cabin behind the tree was not just in disrepair; it was in shambles. The windows were broken out, the front door was falling off its hinges, and a large section of roof was completely missing. Grace tiptoed up the rickety steps and pushed on the door. When it wouldn't budge, she pressed her shoulder against the wood and gave it a good shove. The door fell completely off its hinges, crashing to the floor in a plume of dust and scattered leaves.

When the dust finally settled, Grace stepped into the cabin. The interior of the cabin looked worse than the outside; clearly no one had lived there since her own family had been forced to leave.

I never thought I'd ever be back here again...

Grace took a few tentative steps through the main room, trying not to trip over debris or fall through rotting floorboards. As the breeze blew through the open front door and windows, she stopped in her tracks.

The room seemed to come back to life. She could picture her

mother at the stove cooking supper, and Linnie running around looking for new hiding places; her sisters Rhoda and Rebecca were setting the table, and there, in the corner, sat Will, poring over a book.

Then, just as quickly, those wonderful memories vanished, replaced with frightening ones of their last day in that house. How scared they were when they heard that early morning knock on the door, the fearful sound of the nun slapping Linnie across the face before she emptied Grace's pockets and threw her precious blocks across the room.

The blocks…

In a flash, the room returned to its current state of shambles. Grace picked her way through the rubble to where the old hutch once stood. She knelt down and pushed on the floorboards until one finally budged. And just as she had done eighteen years ago, she pried it up and peered down into the bleak hole beneath the house. She could see nothing, so she reached in with her gloved hand. Her fingertips felt something solid and square, and she pulled it up from the hole.

There it is!

She brushed off the dirt, using her dress to wipe off all the years of grime. There were the painted roses on one side and the letters "G" and "R." In her mind's eye it looked just as it had that Christmas morning when she had pulled her Poppa's blocks from her stocking.

"I said I'd be back for you one day," she whispered. "I just didn't think it would take this long."

She reached back into the hole to find the other blocks, but all she found was dust. Only one had survived. She wrapped it in her handkerchief and slipped it into her pocket. When she stood up, she felt somehow taller, more self-assured. As she looked around the room for the last time, all the childhood memories gave way to a new sense of certainty – that this trip had not been a mistake.

With her head held high, she walked out of the cabin, past the old maple tree. She put her gloved hand on its trunk for just a moment. Her other hand clutched the block in her pocket. Just like that old tree, Grace had grown stronger through every ordeal. Like the tree, she stood tall and graceful, with the dignity that comes from overcoming great suffering.

As she walked to the waiting horse and buggy, her mind was suddenly clear. She couldn't wait to get back to Erie, to her new favorite place in the world: the arms of her future husband. She gave the block a little squeeze and smiled. This time she would take it with her.

CHAPTER FORTY-EIGHT

John's sisters, Florence and Loretta, had done a splendid job planning their brother's wedding and the reception that would follow. The church was filled with the fragrance of hundreds of pink carnations and white roses, and the entire Haibach clan was there, including nephews, nieces, second cousins, in-laws and maiden aunts. Several of the family's business associates and most of Erie's social elite had arrived to celebrate this joyous day. Andy Montgomery was there to serve as best man, and Meg had taken the train from Pittsburgh to be Grace's maid of honor.

But that morning, Grace did not feel altogether well. She put this down to her excitement about this day, the most important day of her life. As she prepared to put on her wedding dress, she tried to shake off the headache that had been growing since she'd opened her eyes that morning. Her forehead felt hot to the touch, but when she looked at herself in the mirror, she was pleased to see her cheeks were especially rosy.

It's just nerves, she said to herself.

When she put on the pearl earrings that Meg had given her, she noticed some tenderness behind her ears but shrugged it off. It was her wedding day, and nothing was going to ruin it.

"Why didn't you let me know you needed a dress?" said Meg, coming into the dressing room. She looked cool, calm and self-possessed in her pale gown; it was a modest design, the color of sea-foam, with high lace collar and lace cuffs. The soft green color brought out the bright green that blazed in her eyes like cut emeralds. "I could have easily ordered you something from Boston!"

The wedding dress was not a Paris original, or even an imitation. It was, in fact, designed and handmade by John's eldest sister. Lena prided herself on being one of Erie's finest dressmakers and insisted that she understood her soon-to-be sister-in-law's taste and style. She had not even remotely succeeded. Although the satin and lace were the finest available, the style seemed to be from the previous century, befitting a much older woman.

"I was busy and not paying attention to the wedding," Grace confessed. "John's twin sisters did all of the planning and his sister Lena made the dress. She wanted it to be a surprise."

"Oh, what a lovely thought. And it should have stopped there!" Meg retorted. She grabbed a box of pins and began cinching in the waist, then stepped back to look at her work. "Oh, dear." Besides being too loose and baggy, this creation had layer upon layer of lace, giving no hint that there might be a slim and shapely figure within. Attached to the front was a large lace bow.

"I guess wearing your slate blue gown down the aisle is out of the question?" asked Meg. She already knew the answer. "The bodice is poorly constructed. And what are *these*?"

She snipped off all the satin ribbons that had been sewn into the bodice and dangled down to the hem of the dress. Then she ripped the big lace bow off the front of the dress. Grace felt too light-headed to protest. Besides, she knew from experience that when Meg took charge, there was no stopping her.

"There. Now at least you have a waist. Just don't move around too much!" said Meg as she gave the fabric one more tug and pinned it snugly in place.

The girls admired Grace's reflection in the mirror. "Much better," said Meg. "Are you carrying a bouquet?"

"No," said Grace. "I was just going to carry a white prayer book, a gift from John's mother. It's my something old."

Meg wrinkled her nose. A white prayer book was simply not acceptable; a bride must always carry a bouquet. She plucked several buds from a small vase of white roses that was sitting on the dressing table, took the satin ribbons she'd cut from the dress and tied the rosebuds into the ribbons. Then she placed the ribbons within the pages of the white prayer book. The ribbons and roses streaming down to the floor gave the prayer book a simple, yet elegant look.

What talent and style, thought Grace. *Will I ever have her flair?*

"That's about all we can do at this point," said Meg. "Unless you want to postpone the wedding a couple of months and wait for a Paris original."

Grace looked at her friend and smiled with gratitude. The first notes of the pipe organ began to fill the church.

"Isn't that our cue?" Meg asked.

And so, at eleven o'clock on a bright spring morning in 1914,

Grace walked down the aisle of St. Mary's Catholic Church. She walked alone, head held high, savoring the fragrance of her beloved pink carnations. She insisted there would be no one to give her away. As she passed each row of guests, she could hear *oohs* and *ahhs* and found herself actually enjoying the attention. It occurred to her that the last time she had been in such a large crowd of well-dressed people was the Montgomery party where she'd met John Haibach. She noticed that the older Haibach women were dressed in dark, somber colors, while the younger ones, John's sisters and nieces, wore lighter, brighter colors – but not too bright. It was as if all the women had taken an unspoken oath not to detract from the beautiful bride. As Grace passed the front pew, she saw that Mary Haibach had forsaken her traditional charcoal grey dresses in favor of a navy blue heavy silk design, gathered about the waist. Grace smiled inwardly: *Who knew John's mother had a waist?*

Just as she reached the altar and her handsome fiancé, the final chord of *The Wedding March* bellowing from the pipe organ, she heard a loud gasp from someone in the front pew. Her confidence deserted her and she lowered her head and stared at the floor. John reached over and took hold of her arm.

Their eyes met, and her self-assurance was restored by his warm smile and firm hand. Still, she couldn't help wondering who had let out such a gasp, and why. *Was it someone from my past?* She looked out over the congregation, seeing familiar faces, but she knew there would be many people there she did not know. Then her eye fastened on the stained glass window set high in the polished brick wall above the church's massive doors. Golden light streamed through the Virgin

Mary's halo, and Grace felt reassured. *If I put my faith in her right now, she will protect me from untoward surprises.*

The ceremony itself went by in a blur. Grace barely heard the voice of the priest. John had to squeeze her hand to prompt her when it was her turn to say "I do." It wasn't reluctance on Grace's part; she wanted this marriage more than anything in the world. Rather, it seemed as though her ears weren't working. Everything sounded muffled and so far away.

"I do," she said. She may have said it twice, she wasn't sure.

"I now pronounce you man and wife," intoned the priest.

As if seeking confirmation, Grace looked out at all the people in the church, at John's family and their friends, seeing all the beaming faces. A few of the women were dabbing their eyes with white handkerchiefs when the church organist launched into the Recessional.

CHAPTER FORTY-NINE

Before John and Grace could exit the front doors of St. Mary's, they were approached by a small gentleman in a striped suit and bowler hat. Grace's heart skipped a few beats. She looked questioningly at her new husband.

"Oh, Harry, how good to see you," said John, shaking the man's hand. "Grace, this is my old friend from high school, Harry Mortensen. Harry's a professional photographer and I've hired him to take our wedding pictures."

Grace let out an audible sigh of relief. The photographer led the couple into a small anteroom in the church and had them sit on an overstuffed settee. However, when the photographer flashed his powder, Grace was not smiling. It hurt too much. Her husband, however, was grinning from ear to ear.

Time was moving so quickly; she felt as though she were on a ride that was ever gaining momentum. Before she knew it, she and her new husband were back at his mother's home for the reception dinner, surrounded by a bevy of Haibach family friends and well-wishers and an endless array of German dishes especially prepared by Mary Haibach's cook. The doors at the rear of the house were open and guests flowed from the living room to the garden, where they admired the roses and seated themselves at small round tables. Grace felt as if she were in a trance as she wandered through the throng of guests, each of whom wanted to hug her or shake her hand.

"I'm sorry I startled you at the church, Grace," said John's sister Lena, giving her a quick embrace. "I just can't believe how beautiful you look in my dress. You make it look so much more glamorous than it did on the dressmaker's dummy!"

"Oh, was that you?" Grace was more relieved to hear that compliment than anyone could know.

"Yes, dear, I couldn't contain myself. You must teach me everything you know about fashion and style."

Grace let out a hearty laugh even though her neck and jaw felt like they were gripped in a vise. Suddenly she found Meg at her side, and the two friends clasped hands.

"Your mother has such a lovely home," said Meg to Lena. "And how charming to have hired a string quartet. Was that your idea?"

Once again Grace thanked her lucky stars that her oldest, dearest friend was at her side to supply just the right remarks and smooth out the conversational rough edges.

"No, actually that was John's idea," said Lena, blushing slightly. "I wish I had thought of it, but I was so busy sewing Grace's gown.... Well, it really took up all of my time."

"And you did a wonderful job, too," said Meg, curling her fingers tightly around Grace's hand.

Andy stood in the doorway and clapped his hands loudly. "May I have your attention, ladies and gentlemen? I know Mary Haibach's garden is the pride of Erie, but I must ask you all to come inside now. Mr. and Mrs. John Haibach are about to cut the cake!"

John, who hadn't stopped beaming since the wedding ceremony, slipped through the crowd and took his wife's arm. "Excuse me, Meg. I must claim my bride."

On a large round table in the middle of the living room stood the biggest cake Grace had ever seen, four tiers tall and swathed in white butter-cream frosting and pink rosettes. On the top tier was a spun-sugar canopy, beneath which stood miniature figurines of a bride and groom. The string quartet began to play the Allegro from Haydn's Opus 64, appropriately called "The Lark," and the wedding guests fairly danced their way into the living room to crowd around Grace and John.

Andy Montgomery rose to his feet and raised his glass. The string quartet fell silent as all eyes and ears turned expectantly to the best man.

"John and Grace, it has been an honor to witness and be part of your wedding. It was also my distinct privilege to be present on the day you two met. Who could have guessed that my twenty-first birthday party would have resulted in not one, but two engagements?" He nodded and winked in Meg's direction and Meg returned her most glorious smile. "I wish you every joy and happiness as you go forth into your new life together!"

Everyone raised a glass and the room was filled with cheers and heartfelt congratulations to the happy couple. Grace so wanted to be present for this, the most joyful day of her life, but she felt oddly detached. Her hearing had gotten worse and a dull ache had settled over her brow. She glanced over at Meg and Andy standing arm in arm, their glasses raised in her honor. John handed her a glass and looked deeply into her eyes. "Here's to you and to us, my love."

She smiled at him and took one small sip of champagne. A sharp stab of pain shot through her throat and up into her ears. John watched his bride's face twist with agony. "Gracie, what is it?"

"I guess I'm just not used to champagne," she answered, clutching the side of her neck.

He leaned over to give her a kiss on the cheek. "You're burning up. You have a fever."

CHAPTER FIFTY

Grace Haibach spent her wedding night tucked under the covers in an upstairs bedroom at her mother-in-law's house. Her temperature was almost 103, and her cheeks were swollen like those of a hamster storing food for the winter.

"It's unusual to see mumps in an adult," said the doctor. "Most often it is children who contract the disease. Your wife must not have been raised around many children growing up."

"She was an only child," said John.

Boy, did he have that wrong! If Grace could have laughed, she would have, but her whole head hurt too much. Even opening her mouth was agony.

"Don't try to talk, darling," said John. "And don't worry, I had mumps when I was young. I won't catch it from you." He smiled reassuringly and squeezed his wife's hand.

"She may feel worse in the next couple of days," the doctor continued. "But the fever will break and the swelling will subside, and she'll start to feel better. There is no remedy for mumps, unfortunately; it just needs to run its course."

He turned to Grace, who was propped up against three pillows, the blankets pulled up to her chin. "Stay indoors and avoid citrus juice and alcohol, which will only irritate the glands and make it more painful."

"So no more champagne, Gracie," said John.

Grace tried to smile at her husband's joke, but the effort hurt her jaw too much. And then it came to her,

My babies came down with mumps a couple nights ago, so I been up with them for two days...

Flo! The exhausted girl in her father's store who had done her a favor, offering her a quick escape from that sad, awkward visit.

Well, I did get to see the old cabin... I found my block... I said good-bye...

Grace drifted off into a fevered sleep.

John slept in a chair at her bedside, and the newlyweds remained at his mother's house until Grace felt well enough to move into their new apartment, not far from where she had stayed with his twin sisters. John had done well: the place was beautifully furnished, with every convenience a just-married couple would need to set up housekeeping.

"It's a good thing we hadn't planned a honeymoon," he said, after they'd settled in. "But I think we could both use one. Where would you like to go?"

Grace replied without hesitation. "Cincinnati."

John thought she was joking; he was expecting Niagara Falls, or maybe New York City. He even thought she might propose a trip to Europe, which he'd have to veto due to the political instability and danger overseas; the First World War had just begun.

"The Cincinnati Zoo, to be precise."

243

John began to laugh but stopped when he saw that his wife was completely serious.

"I didn't know you liked animals," he replied.

"I don't know that I do, but I've never been to a zoo. Let's find out, shall we?"

John had never seen her so excited. "Well then, my love, to the zoo we shall go."

In truth, Grace had always wanted to visit that particular zoo because of a young boy she'd met at the orphanage. All he'd been able to talk about was the time his father took him to the Cincinnati Zoo, the wild animals he had seen and how much fun he'd had. He hadn't known that it would be the last time he would see his father; soon afterwards the child had been dumped at St. Joseph's Orphan Asylum. But in young Grace's mind, that Cincinnati Zoo had seemed a fabulous place; she'd vowed she would visit it one day. Now her chance had come.

"I do believe I am the luckiest man in the world to have found you," said John, wrapping his arms around his wife. "Unpretentious, simple, and yet so lovely, all in one."

And so John and Grace Haibach honeymooned in Cincinnati and they went to the zoo. It probably would have been more exciting if she had been ten years old, but Grace enjoyed the new experience. Her husband never questioned how it was that his cultured young bride from Boston had never been to a zoo.

Thankfully, Grace never had to explain to her husband or anyone else how she got the mumps. It was all in the past. Her new life had begun.

CHAPTER FIFTY-ONE

The true story of Grace Dodson Haibach might have ended there, were it not for the Internet, its almost limitless potential for gathering information, and an innocent question.

"Grandma, you're not going to believe what I found searching the Internet. Do you think these people were distant relatives?"

It was 1990, and my grandmother was ninety-seven years old. She looked at least thirty years younger: her complexion was creamy and smooth, her cheeks were rosy, and her hair was still the color of wheat, thanks to weekly appointments with Lady Clairol. She still had a slim figure – perhaps because of the girdle she insisted on wearing every day – and her posture was ramrod straight.

"Searching the what?"

"The Internet."

She looked at me blankly.

"Never mind about the Internet, I'll explain all about that later." I pulled a stack of papers from my briefcase. "I found this old newspaper article from *The Brookville Republic*. It's dated 1896. It's about these two brothers, William and Frank Dodson, who apparently murdered a Jewish peddler. Any relation to us? It's a wild story."

She stared at me; the roses faded from her cheeks and her slate blue eyes darkened. "No! No relation! Why are you meddling in things that don't concern you?"

She stood up abruptly and the color rushed back into her face. "You need to go. I'm tired and I'm going to bed."

"But, Grandma, it's only six o'clock. I thought we were having dinner together."

She stormed out of the kitchen and headed for the staircase. "Help yourself. Lock the door behind you." Her voice was like ice.

I heard the bedroom door slam shut and the whole house seemed to grow cold. I stood in the middle of the kitchen, perplexed and confused. I didn't know what to do. The table was set for two and the pot on the stove was simmering with beef stroganoff, my favorite dish. The strange ache in the pit of my stomach turned to hunger, and I made myself a plate. Sitting at the kitchen table, I listened in vain for sounds from upstairs, hoping Grandma would come back down.

I waited for over an hour, then washed the pans and dishes and put everything away. Sick at heart, I walked through the hall that led from the kitchen to the front door. There in the hallway, my eye fastened on the pair of old portraits that had hung there since before I was born.

The photos had been taken when my grandmother was eighteen or nineteen years old, commissioned by my Grandfather, who had died long ago. She wore a demure yet stylish silk dress that accented her slender waist. One arm was draped gracefully across her lap. The two photographs had been taken at the same sitting, for she was wearing the same dress. In one she wore a wide brimmed hat trimmed in feathers. In the other picture, her head was bare. Either way, she was beautiful; her face looked serene, her mouth hinting that she was moments away from a smile. But her eyes were strangely hollow and hard.

Grandma had never liked having her picture taken. I knew this by the time I was seven or eight years old, because someone in the family – especially on holidays – always wanted to try out the new camera and snap a group shot. Grandma would make every excuse not to be in the picture. When she was finally persuaded, against her will, she'd stand stiffly until the shutter clicked, a stern expression on her face. In every family photo, her eyes looked vacant and wary.

I had often stared at those portraits when I was a small boy, hoping my grandmother would smile back at me. Now I gave them one last look before locking the front door.

"Maybe," I thought to myself, "I'm finally going to find out what's going on behind those eyes."

It began as curiosity, a simple quest to find out if anyone in the family was related to English royalty or perhaps to one of America's early presidents or founding fathers. The Internet had made genealogical research much easier; my brother's wife had traced her family back to pre-Civil War days, and each bit of information became a piece of the puzzle of who she was. Everyone wants to know where they came from, and if the facts are collected somewhere, why not dig them up? I'd found the article from *The Brookville Republic* completely by accident when I'd been sitting at the computer, idly typing in family surnames.

The next day, I drove back to my grandmother's house in the Los Feliz section of Los Angeles, a neighborhood of stately Tudor,

French Normandy and Mediterranean style homes nestled in the shadow of the Griffith Observatory. My grandparents had lived there since they had come to California in 1928, although I'd never known my Grandpa, who passed away in 1937. Grandma's house had been my favorite place to be ever since I was little. Even now, as an adult, I was accustomed to speaking with her on the phone every day, sometimes several times a day. She was, in fact, the only person in my family to whom I felt especially close.

I had already called her house several times that morning, but there was no answer. Worried, unable to concentrate on work, I left my office in downtown Los Angeles to investigate.

I knocked on the door and rang the bell. When she didn't answer, I used my key to let myself in. She was sitting on the sofa in the living room, staring out the big picture window.

"Grandma, are you all right?"

I bent to give her a kiss, but she turned her head away.

"Please talk to me! What's this about?"

Finally, after an interminable silence, she turned and glared at me. "You have no right to dig into my past. Who the *hell* do you think you are?"

I'd never heard Grandma curse before.

"I wasn't digging into your past, Grandma. I was just researching our family tree. What's the big deal?"

She was breathing hard and twisting the rosary beads in her hand. She looked at me with an expression I had never seen before: hatred.

"I have spent my entire life trying to escape my past." She

spoke each word slowly and deliberately as her eyes filled with tears. "And I have not come this far for you to destroy it all over again."

I didn't know what to say. How could she think her own grandson, who loved her so dearly, would try to destroy her?

"You promise me," she demanded, her eyes boring into mine, "that what I am about to tell you stays between us!"

She turned her face away as tears streamed down her cheeks. This was the first time I'd ever seen her cry.

"I promise." I would have said anything to stop her tears.

After a long moment, she pulled out the cotton lace handkerchief she always kept tucked into her sleeve and dabbed her eyes. "I'm not who you think I am," she whispered.

CHAPTER FIFTY-TWO

According to the story I had heard my entire life, my grandmother was an only child, born in Boston to wealthy parents who were killed in a train accident when she was just sixteen. She had married my grandfather and given birth to three boys, my father and my two uncles, in Erie, Pennsylvania, before the family had moved to Los Angeles on account of Grandpa's heart condition. Grandpa had switched from the meatpacking business to automotive repairs and had run three successful garages before succumbing to a heart attack in 1937, dying in my grandmother's arms at the young age of forty-seven.

That was all I knew. I had never questioned it. Grace Dodson Haibach, our family's matriarch, was a beautiful, dignified lady, a pillar of her community and her church, admired and respected by all. Stern but kind, she always seemed as if she were holding herself in reserve. I'd never seen her show outward signs of affection toward my father or my uncles. I was, in fact, the only member of the family to enjoy the warmth she could display.

I didn't return to the office that day.

That afternoon, our bond was put to the test. We sat in her living room, the sheaf of newspaper clippings from almost a century ago resting on the sofa between us like an unwanted guest.

"Michael, run upstairs to my room. In my closet, way in the

back on the top shelf, hidden behind all the hatboxes, there's a small gold gift box. Do not open it! Just bring it down here to me."

The last time I'd tried to go in that closet, I'd gotten in big trouble. I was eight years old and bored, and Grandma was outside in her garden. After making sure the coast was clear, I ran up to her room, pretending I was a spy on a covert mission into forbidden territory: Grandma's bedroom. I tried the closet door and it opened just a crack before it seemed to get stuck. I gave it a hard yank and the knob jerked from my hand as the door slammed shut. There was my grandmother, towering over me. She didn't say a word; she didn't have to. The look on her face said it all.

This time was different; I had permission. I opened the closet door and found everything in perfect order, all her clothes lined up neatly and organized by style and color. On the top closet shelf were a dozen hatboxes. I pulled them down and spied an old-fashioned gift box with a hinged lid. I was sorely tempted to open it then and there, but even though the suspense was almost killing me, I grabbed it and raced back down the stairs.

"Here it is, Grandma."

She smiled as she took the box and lifted the lid, shielding its contents from my view.

"This is the picture they took of us the day we entered the orphans' home."

She passed me a tattered, old sepia-colored photograph of three unhappy children in plaid dresses. I stared at their angry little faces.

"This one is me," she said, pointing to the smaller girl in the plaid dress. The hurt, angry, wary look in her eyes reminded me of something. I looked up into Grandma's face and thought of the twin black and white portraits that hung in the hallway. Then I understood: the look in her eyes was fear, fear and tragedy that could not have been spoken about until now.

The whole house seemed to sigh with relief as she began to tell me the story, every detail recalled with clarity as if it had just happened yesterday. She told me of her early life in the backwoods of Pennsylvania, what had happened to her father and mother, how she and her siblings ended up at St. Joseph's, the tortures she had endured, and her escape to the Brownings' house in Pittsburgh. She told me about meeting Meg Browning hiding under the bedclothes and the instant friendship they formed – a friendship that, without her wanting or willing it, forged the design of my grandmother's new life. She told me how, through Meg's endless coaching and maneuvering, she had met and married my grandfather, and how she'd managed to track down her remaining family before the wedding. How she had become a lady, a society lady, and firmly shut the door on her past.

After she had finished, we sat in silence.

"What else is in the box?" I said at last.

I wanted her to just hand it over so that I could rifle through its contents. Instead she clicked the lid shut and grinned mischievously. She was toying with me and I knew it, but I would let her take her time. After all, her secrets had stayed hidden for almost a hundred years; what would a few more minutes matter?

She lifted the lid again. As she stared into the box, sadness crept back into her face.

"This was Will's." She gently placed her brother's rosary in my hand. The metal had tarnished, but the mother-of-pearl beads glistened in the afternoon sun that streamed through the picture window. "You guard it now." She closed my fingers around the rosary. I wondered if any of the prayers said over those beads had ever been answered.

We sat in silence, each absorbed in private thoughts. Finally I found the courage to speak.

"May I ask you something, Grandma?"

She looked as if she were far, far away. I did not want to interrupt her private reverie, but there was something else I needed to know, and I touched her arm gently.

"Yes, certainly," she said, snapping back into the present.

"Did Grandpa ever know? I mean, did you ever tell him what really happened to you?"

She stared out the window for a long moment.

"I suspect he may have known. But if he did know, he never let on. You know he died in my arms."

I'd heard her say that many times before, but listened intently now as she told me the rest of the story.

She had heard John's car pull into the driveway, surprised that he was home earlier than usual. She waited for the cheerful "Gracie, I'm home!", the greeting she always heard when he came home from work, but nothing came. Sensing that something was not right, she ran down the stairs to the foyer, where she found her husband sitting on the wooden bench, his back leaning heavily against the wall.

"John, what's wrong? You look flushed." She sat down next to him and put her hand on his brow.

He answered in a weak voice. "I'm just tired, I think."

Grace ran her hand against his cheek. His skin felt warm and clammy. "Well, let's get you upstairs. You have plenty of time for a nap before dinner."

She helped him to his feet but he was having difficulty walking. "I think I'll just lie down in the study," he said.

Grace guided him to the sofa in his study and placed a pillow under his head. "Just rest," she said, kissing him gently on the forehead. "I'll make you some tea."

"You're so good to me, Gracie. I'll be fine in a minute or two."

Grace stood for a moment in the doorway and watched her husband close his eyes. *He'll be fine,* she said to herself, *he just needs to rest. A nap and a cup of tea will surely help.* She went to the kitchen, turned on the stove, and stood there for ten minutes, silently cursing the water for not boiling faster.

When she came back to the study with the cup and saucer in her hand, he was fast asleep. She sat down next to him and patted his cheek. He neither stirred nor opened his eyes. She grabbed his shoulders and gave him a shake. When he still didn't move, she began to panic and took him in her arms. It was then, when she hugged him close, that she heard the death rattle – a guttural shudder that came from deep within his chest.

"Dear God!" she cried, as she pulled him even closer. "Please don't take him from me now! Why must you take everyone I love from me?"

John Haibach, forty-seven years of age, had died of a massive heart attack. Grace was now a widow at the age of forty-three, with three teenage sons to raise alone.

I wanted to reach out and take her hand, but she sat as still as a stone with her handkerchief at her lips.

"I cried for months. My whole life changed in that one horrible moment. I didn't even get the chance to say goodbye."

Her eyes brimmed over with tears, and I took her hand in mine. I couldn't think of any words of comfort and could only squeeze her hand. Then the tears stopped, and my grandmother's face resumed its usual composure. She looked deep into my eyes.

"I know he loved me. After we were married, he never, *ever* asked me about my past."

She reached for the gold box and pulled a small card from the very bottom.

"What's this, Grandma?"

"This is the first birthday card your grandfather gave me the year after we were married. Read it."

I stared at the writing on the card.

"Aloud, please," she prompted.

"My darling Grace," I read, "Happy Birthday! There isn't anything you could say that would ever change my love for you. I hope you know that. Your adoring husband, John."

The illusion was perfect. Why question it? Why scratch the surface of something that was so good, so genuine, and so rewarding for both of them? Their love was real, even if the facts were not.

"When I received letters from Linnie, I read them and burned them. There was no point in keeping them."

"What about your father? Did you ever hear from him again?"

Grace squared her shoulders and sat up a little straighter. "I did. Shortly after I buried your grandfather, I received a letter from him. He'd read the obituary. Aside from sending condolences, he had the nerve to ask if he could come live with us in California. I guess he thought I'd have extra room now that I had just buried my husband. He also suggested that his three grandchildren needed to get to know their grandfather."

That seemed to irk her the most. "Well! I had only seen him once in forty years. I didn't even *know* him. And to say he now wanted to get to know his grandchildren – they didn't even know he existed."

"It sounds like he was trying to reach out."

"He should have tried that when I was twelve and prayed for him to rescue me. Besides, I had my hands full, dealing with your grandfather's death and his businesses. And I had three sons to protect. It would have been awkward to have my dead father return to the living. I didn't want to start lying to my boys."

"So how did you respond?"

"I didn't."

Clearly, she had not forgotten, nor had she forgiven.

I was, at first, disappointed to learn this. But then I saw the pieces of her life falling neatly into place. It takes strength to create a lie and live an entire life behind it. It suddenly dawned on me that my grandmother had shrewdly gathered information from the examples of her early life. This strict, proper, upright lady took her cue from Mrs.

Browning, another woman widowed in her prime – a woman who had taken control of her emotions and her household, who never showed any chinks in her armor.

"And what happened to Meg and Andy?"

Her face turned ashen. "Meg," she sighed. "Meg was my guardian angel. She and Andy married about a year after your grandfather and I. We didn't go to their wedding; I was pregnant with your Uncle Don and dealing with complications. Your grandfather insisted we not chance traveling to Pittsburgh for their big day. I didn't protest too much. I was afraid and couldn't risk being recognized by Meg's mother.

"A year later Meg was pregnant; she had worse complications than I did. She died in childbirth. They saved the baby. It was a little girl and they named her Gracie. I never did get to see her. Andy was so distraught over her death that he left the baby with parents and traveled the world. Your grandfather would get postcards from him from some of the strangest places – Tanzania, Morocco, India. Then suddenly the postcards stopped coming.

"I still think of Meg almost every day, wondering how she would have handled this or that situation. Funny… I guess I am still learning from Meg. I still hear her voice."

"I would have liked her," I said. Grandma simply nodded, as if to say, *Of course you would.*

"And there's this," she said, reaching into the box and pulling out an old chunk of wood. She put it in my hand. The block was no longer square and the painted letters were gone. I could barely make out the faded painted roses.

CHAPTER FIFTY-THREE

I continued to dig into my grandmother's past. Part of me still wanted validation that the whole incredible tale was true. Grace Haibach had, after all, created a new identity based on other people's lives. I still wondered how much of her confession had really happened. I didn't want to doubt her, or to upset the delicate balance of trust that had been so painful to establish. I just wanted to know more.

"Your story is so amazing, Grandma," I told her one afternoon as we sat in her sunlit kitchen drinking iced tea and nibbling on cookies she had just taken from the oven. "It really ought to be told."

She stood up abruptly and the old, cold fire sprang into her eyes. It was the same look she had given me when she caught me misbehaving when I was a little boy, the same look she had given when I first asked about that article in the *Brookville Republic*.

"No! No one must know of this until after I'm dead."

I was crestfallen; I had not expected such a vehement reaction. Then she placed a gentle hand on my shoulder.

"There are people still alive who might be hurt. I could not bear that to happen."

"But Grandma," I pleaded, trying to think of a few good reasons that might persuade her to change her mind.

"I said no." Her voice was low and firm, as if she were talking to a ten-year-old. She sat down again at the table. "It's all right, I guess, if you want to continue all this research you've started. I certainly can't stop you, now that you've gotten in over your head."

She chuckled, and I was relieved she wasn't angry with me.

"However," she continued, "you will not write one single word until after I'm gone."

"I promise." I crossed my heart and raised my right hand.

Census data, newspaper archives and letters to the orphanage confirmed many of the facts, but it was the Jefferson County Historical Society in Pennsylvania that led me to the motherlode.

Mrs. William McCracken, the local historian, was willing to continue the research for the modest fee of five dollars an hour. In her mid-seventies, she still lived on her family's property, which turned out to be directly across the creek from the old Dodson property. Even more uncannily, she was a direct descendant of William McCracken, one of the lawyers who had defended William and Frank Dodson at the trial that ended in their manslaughter conviction on that Christmas Eve of 1896.

I couldn't wait to tell Grandma what Mrs. McCracken had found.

"I'm a little disturbed you're paying this woman five dollars an hour," Grace told her grandson when he arrived to share the revelation. "It's too much money."

"Well, it beats flying back there and doing it myself," I replied.

"I suppose. But not as much fun." She smiled. "So what's this new revelation?"

Mrs. McCracken had located a tape recording made in the late 1960s or early 1970s. Her uncle, an old man by then, had been persuaded to record his recollection for the Jefferson County Historical Society's archives. He had known several of William Dodson's brothers and sisters.

"Her uncle worked at a Brockaway sawmill when he was young – the same sawmill where the Dodson boys worked. On the tape, he tells the story of a millworker who boasted to his coworkers that he and a buddy had been the ones who killed the Jewish peddler. The peddler that William and Frank had been convicted of murdering."

My grandmother's expression did not change. She just stared at me for a long moment. "Go on," she said calmly.

"The man remembered the incident caused quite a commotion among the mill workers when they heard this guy's confession. He said he was 'ridding the world of yet one more piece of trash,' and he got away with it because he let some poor saps take the rap. That's what he said on the tape, Grandma."

I had expected some sort of reaction, but there was none. She nodded her head slightly, but her face remained stoic.

"Well, before the authorities could be called in to investigate, the real murderer died in a freak accident at the mill. The people who ran the sawmill never documented the confession or investigated the accident. They never even told the authorities. They just let it go down as one of those unfortunate fatalities, the kind that used to happen at places like that."

I wanted to believe the accident was no accident. It could have been suicide, but my gut told me otherwise. After all, it was one of the mills where the Dodson brothers had found employment, and they might have still had relatives and friends working there.

"I guess they figured, 'what's the point?' With the real murderer dead, the damage had already been done and what would it accomplish now? Destroy yet another family?"

"Why are you telling me this?" my grandmother snapped.

Her anger surprised me and took me aback. *Was she missing the point?*

"Well, William and Frank always denied committing the murder, right? So this is further proof of their innocence."

"I already *know* that," she shot back, as if I were the one who had missed the point. "I told you they didn't do it. My father could never have killed anyone."

I had had visions of clearing my great-grandfather's name, but I knew the tape-recorded story fell short of being concrete proof. It was hearsay, but it qualified as "monumental hearsay." However, I could sense that my grandmother was just the tiniest bit relieved to have her father's innocence confirmed.

EPILOGUE

A few years after Grace Haibach revealed her real life to me, her mind started to deteriorate, requiring full-time care. To keep her in the family home she loved so much, we tried round-the-clock nursing care. This brought its own struggle, as my grandmother viewed each nurse as an intruder and invader of her privacy. Just before her hundredth birthday, she fell and broke her hip. We had to move her into an assisted living facility, where she lived another three years, always wanting to return to her own home. At one hundred and three, she passed away peacefully in her sleep.

The morning after she died, I stopped by the old home in Los Feliz. The house and garden were still maintained, but minimally — not in the way Grandma would have liked. As I stood in front of the house where so many secrets had been guarded for so long, I remembered one brilliant Saturday morning about a year after my grandmother's confession, when I had dropped by her house unannounced. The sky was clear blue and the warmth of the sun was invigorating. The house itself was open like a flower in full bloom — every door and window flung wide. I hadn't seen her air out the house like this in years.

I found her in the backyard, on her knees in a far corner of the garden. She was planting rose bushes around her garden's newest addition – a newly planted sapling.

"Grandma!" I called.

She looked up from under her large straw hat and broke into a huge smile. "Michael!"

I savored that moment: my grandmother on her knees, trowel in hand, her radiant smile.

"What are you doing? Where did that come from?"

"Do you like it?" She slowly stood up and pointed at the little tree. "This part of the garden always needed something. What do you think? I always wanted a maple tree of my own."

For a moment I thought about that stately old maple in the Pennsylvania woods and wondered if it was still thriving. Someday this little tree would be just as strong and stately.

"Are you hungry? How about some lunch?"

"You still have one rose left to plant," I said, pointing toward the rosebush lying on the ground.

"Oh, leave it for the gardener."

"Let me plant it. You go start lunch," I said, taking the trowel from her hand.

"If you like," she replied, pulling off her work gloves and handing them to me.

She had already dug the hole. I removed the plastic bag that protected its roots and carefully placed it in the ground, packing the dirt around it. Just as I finished, a gentle breeze whispered through the garden, making the tag hanging from the stem flutter. The photo showed what the flower would look like in full bloom come summer – a large blood-red blossom. The name on the tag was *Deep Secret.*

I spun around and caught a glimpse of my grandmother standing by the back door watching me. The moment our eyes met, she ducked into the house.

I turned back to look at the tags on the other roses she had planted. *Meg of My Heart, Prince William, St. John.* The last one I spotted was simply named *Grace*.

Come summer, her garden would be spectacular.

My grandmother's life, according to her, only began after she married my Grandfather. But it was her life before that shaped her character, giving her the strength to move on and not look back. Grace Dodson Haibach survived her times, cleared her past from her mind, and refused to let it control any part of her. Not acknowledging that past to a single soul was her way of surviving. Denial is not necessarily a bad thing if it allows one to survive a soul-destroying experience without losing one's soul; we all know it's the people, experiences and events that shape us into what and who we eventually become.

That, in essence, is what I learned from her story. We are not defined or limited by our experiences; we each have the ability to choose how we deal with what fate hands us. It's those decisions — those choices — that either hold us back or open new doors to a better future.

I never asked her why she had held on to those items in the gold box, but I'm very glad she did.

ABOUT THE AUTHOR

MICHAEL HAIBACH graduated from Pepperdine University with a Bachelor of Science in Marketing & Business Management.

Most of Michael's career has been in marketing and advertising, on both the agency and client sides of the business. He began his career with senior management positions within the financial services industry in Los Angeles.

He then worked for a variety of industries as an in-house marketing director; as well as holding senior management positions with some of the leading advertising agencies in Southern California, successfully elevating the profitability, visibility and performance of a wide variety of industries — from financial services, skin-care & fragrance, airlines, higher education, city governments, non-profits, and even pizza for a national restaurant chain.

Although Michael has written a multitude of advertising copy, and successful marketing and promotion plans over the years, this is his first literary work. Inspired by his grandmother.

75085106R00153

Made in the USA
San Bernardino, CA
24 April 2018